OPPORTUNITIES IN MATHEMATICS
FOR PRIMARY SCHOOLS

Tom Comer

Trentham Books

First published in 1996 by Trentham Books Limited

Trentham Books Limited
Westview House
734 London Road
Oakhill
Stoke-on-Trent
Staffordshire
England ST4 5NP

British Cataloguing in Publication Data
A catalogue record for this book is available from the British Library
ISBN: 1 85856 018 7

Designed and typeset by Trentham Print Design Ltd., Chester
and printed in Great Britain by Bemrose Shafron Ltd, Chester

Contents

TO MARY

INTRODUCTION

The purpose of this book is to:

- provide an overview of the primary mathematics curriculum following the implementation of the National Curriculum and its latest revision

- give some indication of improvements which should be made in the teaching of primary mathematics

- help teachers to ensure that pupils are given their full entitlement to the programmes of study.

The views and opinions expressed in this book are largely my own, formed over many years of advisory and inspection work in local education authorities, both in-service and initial teacher training and, as yet, a limited number of recent primary Ofsted inspections. There is good evidence to support the opinions expressed in the book about standards and matters for concern; for example, the new and welcome information published in the annual review of Ofsted inspections.

It is hoped that the book will prove useful to all primary teachers of whatever phase specialisation, to those undergoing initial training and to experienced practitioners alike. It should also be useful to teachers of secondary pupils in Key Stage 3. The intention is to give an overview of primary mathematics which will be helpful to all.

The transition between key stages leads to discontinuity of experience in mathematics for many pupils. Teachers specialising in one or other of the primary stages do not always have a complete overview of the work done in the earlier or subsequent key stage. Pupils' achievements made in Key Stage 1 are not always sufficiently well built upon in Key Stage 2. Secondary teachers rarely give full credit for, or understand the scope of, the work done in primary schools. In Key Stage 2, part of the difficulty stems from an incomplete view of how children learn mathematics, especially in the earlier years. Consequently teachers are not always effective in providing satisfactory end experience and are less good at diagnosing and remedying pupils' difficulties than they could be.

The text of the book is firmly linked to the content of the programmes of study of the attainment targets. The first part of the book contains background information about the mathematics curriculum, standards of achievement and contributory matters. Much of the second part of the book amplifies specific points and technical matters but the reader is warned that a full treatment of the programmes of study is well beyond the scope of this book.

PART 1
ENTITLEMENT, STANDARDS AND CONTRIBUTORY FACTORS

Entitlement to the curriculum

All pupils have an equal entitlement to the Programmes of Study of the subjects of the National Curriculum. No pupil may be denied access to any part of the statutory curriculum unless a statement of special educational need has been specifically made to that effect. Pupils receive their entitlement when they are given full and equal access to the statutory curriculum at levels which match their age, ability and prior attainment.

Equality of opportunity is not the same as equality of treatment: schools should compensate for disadvantage. Pupils may have a learning difficulty (and therefore a special educational need); language, gender, and cultural differences also have significant effects upon the progress of groups and individuals.

The overwhelming majority of pupils in mainstream schools, including those with special educational needs, are taught the full range of the National Curriculum attainment targets, according to age and ability. In certain circumstances, however, it may be in a pupil's interest for special arrangements to be made to modify the curriculum or exempt the individual from part or the whole of it. Modification of the curriculum for an individual pupil can only be legally effected where a statement of special educational need has been made. Guidance is set out in the Department for Education's Code of Practice for the Identification and Assessment of Special Educational Needs.

Special educational needs are defined in mainstream schools as follows:

> A child has *special educational needs* if he or she has a *learning difficulty* which calls for *special educational provision* to be made for him or her.

A child has a *learning difficulty* if he or she:

* has a significantly greater difficulty in learning than the majority of children of the same age

* has a disability which either prevents or hinders the child from making use of educational facilities of a kind provided for children of the same age in schools within the area of the local education authority

* is under five and falls within the definition of the above or would do if special educational provision were not made for that child. (DFE *Code of Practice on the Identification and Assessment of Special Educational Needs*, 1994)

Special educational provision means any provision which is additional to or in any way different from that available generally for pupils of the same age in maintained schools in the same area (pupils whose first language is other than English are excepted).

Where a pupil's first language differs from that in which he or she will be taught at school (i.e. English or Welsh), this is not a learning difficulty. An ESL pupil (English as a second language) may, however, suffer lack of equality of opportunity in consequence.

In Wales, primary pupils in Welsh-speaking classes are entitled to be and are taught in Welsh; English is not part of the National Curriculum in Key Stage 1 for such pupils. In England, pupils whose first language is other than English, even where they are in a majority, have no entitlement to be taught in their first language. This means that there are many pupils who are effectively learning the subjects of the National Curriculum in a language which is strange to them. Some special provision for pupils whose first language is other than English is available to certain schools from the Home Office to interpret and help pupils to comprehend lessons and texts.

There are many cases where able ESL pupils are given mathematical work which is below their capacity, teachers failing to make a proper distinction between performance in English and ability. Regrettably the only indicator of potential which many schools have is a standardised reading test, whilst in some schools no objective measures are taken at all. On occasions, ESL pupils are incorrectly placed in ability groups or sets and the work contained in a textbook is too low in mathematical level although the pupil may nevertheless find difficulty in the comprehension of the English text. Where this sort of mismatch occurs (and it tends to happen more often where ESL pupils are in a minority), there can be little question that the pupils are denied their right to equality of access to the programmes of study. Schools are expected to compensate for disadvantage so as to give, as far as possible, equality of access and of opportunity. It is essential that decisions relating to ability (the grouping or setting of pupils for example) are made with full and reliable information, using appropriate criteria, such as standardised tests or evaluations of National Curriculum outcomes.

In mathematics, words are used in a more precise way than in everyday speech and the subject has an important additional vocabulary of its own. The difficulties which are thereby presented to all children are compounded in the case of those whose first language is not English.

At one time, girls did less well than boys in most school subjects: the girls were underachieving. We cannot be certain of the causes of gender differences in attainment, but it is very likely that social assumptions, attitudes and economic factors strongly influence differential expectations of boys' and girls' achievement in school. Social attitudes are changing. Young women are less likely to be unemployed than young men. The economic need for women to work and to plan for lifetime careers has increased and their academic achievements have risen commensurately. Steadily, the earlier differences in attainment have been eroded as girls catch up with, and surpass boys. In language-based subjects, girls are already well ahead and, overall, they out-perform boys in the GCSE examinations in nearly all subjects. They have recently taken the lead in science and are now achieving equally with boys in mathematics. Although these changes are true generally, within a given school boys may do better one year and girls in the next. Overall, however, the national trend in favour of girls is plain.

Gender issues are less clear cut than before, but two points are emerging. It is worrying that boys are now tending to achieve less highly than girls, for this suggests a pattern of relative under-achievement by boys similar to the former (of girls). It is also worrying that girls are not capitalising on their success in mathematics and are not taking up Sixth Form A-level courses in similar numbers to boys. At present, boys outnumber girls 2:1 in take-up of A-level despite the level pegging at GCSE (*Science and Mathematics in Schools: a review*, Ofsted, 1994). It is likely that the girls are not shunning maths and science on the grounds that the subjects are difficult, but because other subjects have more appeal for them. If we wish to increase the uptake of university courses in science and technology, then Sixth Form courses in mathematics should be made more attractive to girls.

Examination of samples of pupils' written work shows that girls tend to be more conscientious than boys; the presentation of their written work is better and it is less likely to be unfinished. More needs to be known about the differences in boys' and girls' learning: preferred styles, work habits, their attitudes towards the subject, etc, which contribute to differential attainment.

The Curriculum

The Education Reform Act of 1988, which incorporates the National Curriculum, is the first piece of legislation which defines the substance of a statutory curriculum in this country and brings us into line with many of our neighbours. During the nineteen-sixties, the primary school curriculum as a whole came under pressure for change. The establishment of non-selective comprehensive schools in most local authorities meant that, with the ending of the eleven-plus examination, primary schools had considerable freedom to broaden the curriculum. When no longer necessary for the primaries to prepare their pupils for grammar school entry, the way was clear for a broader range of subjects (although it should not be forgotten that some Local Education Authorities (LEAs) still retain grammar schools and secondary modern schools and the eleven-plus examination). Some squeezing of the time allowed for the subject was inevitable within the broader curriculum. Other factors which were influential in the change in primary mathematics at this time were:

- the metrication of weights and measures and the decimalisation of the currency;

- 'top-down' pressure arising from curriculum innovation in secondary schools;

- 'modern' mathematics, promoted by the teacher training institutions and publishers of texts and schemes.

The old systems of money, Imperial weights and measures, which had given such enormous scope for the practice of mental and written arithmetic, were replaced by the much simpler decimal currency and the metric system. Up to this time, mathematics in most primary schools was predominantly arithmetic, which included the multiplication tables up to twelve, the 'four rules' and problems involving whole numbers and fractions, money (pounds shillings and pence) weights (ounces, pounds, stones, hundredweights, tons), measures (inches, feet, yards, chains, furlongs, miles), fractional parts of quantities, and mensuration (perimeters, areas and volumes of rectangular shapes, capacity).

Until the time of metrication, decimal fractions were rarely introduced to primary school children earlier than the age of ten. The metric system brought a new emphasis upon decimals (decimal money, weights and measures); before then decimals were thought difficult for junior pupils to learn. Today, although difficulties with understanding of place value are widely acknowledged, decimal fractions are prominent in the primary school curriculum.

Other aspects of arithmetic in primary schools began to be questioned; for example, what 'facts' should be learned and known? Was it necessary any longer to remember tables up to twelve times? Was it important to know them at all? Was it really important that children learn to do long division, as generations had done before, without much understanding and which few could remember? These questions are only partly answered in the National Curriculum Order for Mathematics.

In secondary schools, courses were devised by serving teachers who wished to improve the teaching of school mathematics. Grammar school and university teachers agreed that school courses no longer matched the way the subject was treated in the universities. They also felt that mathematics would be easier to understand and the difficulties which the subject presented could be eased if school courses reflected the modern ideas, especially sets and algebraic structure, as unifying elements of the subject. The new mathematics courses of the public schools and grammar schools spread to the comprehensives, and the remaining secondary moderns, through changes in the initial training of teachers, new textbooks and examination syllabuses. In Scotland, by contrast, the main force for change was the school inspectorate.

In the secondary schools, the change in content was sweeping. The old, static geometry derived from Euclid and associated with rote learning of theorems and proofs was replaced by motion geometry based on transformations (translation, reflection, rotation, enlargement, shear,...). Calculus disappeared from the 11-16 course. Other topics new to schools included sets and algebraic structure (linking the subject matter of number, algebra and the new geometry), vectors, matrices, statistics and probability. Much of the new material has not stood the test of time and has disappeared from examination syllabuses and is absent from the National Curriculum programmes of study.

In order to make it accessible to children of average attainment and below, the new material was diluted so that in texts and CSE examination questions the relevance of much of the mathematics to the needs and understanding of the majority of pupils was very doubtful. For example, work with matrix operations and vectors is appropriate for able pupils, but generally out of place for pupils of average ability and below average. Yet CSE examination papers often included questions on topics which could not be understood by the pupils who were to answer them, except in a mechanical way. As the Cockcroft Report made clear, top-down development can distort and unbalance the mathematics of the many whilst serving the interests of the few.

In the primary schools, the stimulus for change was more the decimalisation of the currency and metrication of weights and measures rather than anything else. But, having trimmed down the old arithmetic, schools were ready to broaden the base of the mathematical education of their pupils. Naturally enough, much of the new material matched that of the new mathematics of the secondary schools.

Three important branches of mathematics new to primary schools were identified in the Schools Council Curriculum Bulletin No.1:

- Algebraic Structure, Sets and Logic;
- Probability and Statistics;
- Mathematical Modelling.

Sets and logic, decimals, symmetry, plane and solid shape, statistical diagrams such as block graphs and pictograms became features of primary school classrooms. Courses of initial and in-service training supported new approaches to the teaching of number so that mathematical modelling became part of the fabric of established teaching methodology; for example, the use of structured materials such as multibase arithmetic sets, number tracks, abaci, cubes, Cuisenaire rods and logiblocks. The modelling approach to early number work has stood the test of time. Primary school geometry which, in the form of mensuration (calculation of areas and volumes), had previously been little more than an extension of arithmetic, now received a new look as 'Shape', owing much to the ideas of symmetry and transformations, laying down a foundation for the new dynamic geometry of the secondary schools.

At the outset, the new subject matter of primary mathematics connected with sets, mappings and numbers in bases other than ten, was introduced to improve the effectiveness of teaching and learning of specific concepts – especially in number – rather than to provide the unifying link between branches of the subject which featured in the secondary school courses. However, the purpose of some of it became confused, so that children could be engaged in work at an inappropriate level of abstraction; for example, with sets or doing repetitive exercises in converting numbers from one base to another.

By the mid-eighties, the Government had decided to introduce a national curriculum as part of a package of measures designed to increase public confidence in the capacity of the maintained system of education to deliver good teaching and high standards of achievement, especially in literacy and numeracy. The Government was also concerned about the wide variation in the broader curricular provision; for example, some primary schools taught science whilst others did not and the range of subjects taken by many 14-year-old secondary pupils was often too narrow.

Since 1989, the great majority of primary schools have made good progress in the implementation of the National Curriculum programmes of study and generally meet their statutory obligations.

The revised National Curriculum for mathematics is set out in the document produced by the Department for Education and Welsh Office entitled *Mathematics in the National Curriculum* (HMSO 1995). The document contains the detail of the subject matter and the related assessment objectives. The curriculum has been amended twice since the original version was published in 1989. The current version is expected to remain in force, without further alteration, for a period of at least five years from September, 1995.

For readers unfamiliar with the organisation of the National Curriculum in England and Wales some preliminary explanation is in order. Primary education is divided into two key stages:

Key Stage 1 (pupils aged 5 - 7)
        Year 1 (5 - 6)
        Year 2 (6 - 7)

Key Stage 2 (pupils aged 7 - 11)
        Year 3 (7 - 8)
        Year 4 (8 - 9)
        Year 5 (9 - 10)
        Year 6 (10 - 11)

The National Curriculum does not apply, in the statutory sense, to nursery and reception (R) infant classes although teachers of these classes are likely to pay close attention to the Key Stage 1 curriculum when planning their work.

In England, the subjects included in the National Curriculum for primary schools are English, mathematics, science, technology, information technology, history, geography, art, music and physical education. In Wales, the National Curriculum includes Welsh, English (except in Welsh-speaking classes in Key Stage 1) and the other subjects, as in England. Religious education is also required to be taught in all maintained schools (in consequence of the 1944 Act).

Attainment targets

An attainment target is defined as the knowledge, skills and understanding which pupils are expected to have by the end of each key stage. An attainment target contains the Programme of Study (PoS), which sets out the subject matter required to be taught within a particular key stage.

The three attainment targets Number; Shape, Space and Measures; and Handling Data, contain the subject matter of the curriculum. The attainment target Using and Applying Mathematics provides the framework for practising and communicating the mathematical knowledge in suitable contexts and for developing ideas of argument, proof and generalisation and is intended to link and underpin the work in the other attainment targets.

To achieve necessary breadth, all of the elements of the programmes of study, as defined for each key stage, should be included in the scheme of work; but that does not imply equality of emphasis for each attainment target. In Key Stage 1 and, to a lesser extent in Key Stage 2, the Number and Applications attainment targets should normally receive a greater share of the teaching time.

The programmes of study do not define a rigid order of teaching but schemes of work and the planning of lessons should take account of the need for continuity and progression within each key stage. Although the programme of study is defined for all pupils within a given key stage, subject matter which is defined in earlier or later stages may be taught to individual pupils where they would benefit.

The substance of the original version of the mathematics National Curriculum was put together, in 1988, by a committee, the membership of which was sufficiently broad to guarantee lively disagreement concerning what should be taught. The opportunity was presented at that time for a raising of standards through realistic but rigorous curricular provision for the average pupil, but the opportunity was lost. The original version of the curriculum for primary schools was too ambitious in terms of its breadth but lacked rigour in basic numerical knowledge and skills. The recent revision undertaken by the Schools Curriculum and Assessment Authority (SCAA), in conjunction with national consultation, reduced the scope of the primary mathematics curriculum and clarifies requirements for teaching numerical work and applications, which is welcome.

The review was intended to reduce the burden on teachers by simplifying assessment and reducing the subject content. It was also intended to enable more time to be given where necessary to the basics of the core curriculum, particularly in primary schools, and to facilitate individual school diversification and specialisation; for example, languages, science or the creative and expressive arts.

As a result of the review, the number of mathematics attainment targets was reduced to three in Key Stage 1 and four in Key Stage 2. Some of the primary mathematics was deleted entirely and some was removed from Key Stage 2 to Key Stage 3. Thus, in Key Stage 1, there are three mathematical attainment targets: Using and Applying mathematics; Number; Shape, Space and Measures. In Key Stage 2, there are four: Using and Applying Mathematics; Number; Shape, Space and Measures; Handling Data.

One of the most important features of the review of the curriculum is that the programmes of study are now defined for the key stage rather than a particular level.

Although there have been improvements, many believe that a more determined attempt could have been made to inject more rigour into the teaching of numerical work and applications in Key Stage 2, even at the sacrifice of some breadth. Another weaknesses is that the criteria for achievement of pupils of average and below average ability, as defined in the level descriptions, are low, particularly in arithmetic. As an example, knowledge of multiplication tables up to 10 x 10 is a feature of level 4, attained by the average eleven-year-old whereas

French children are expected to know them by the age of nine (G Howson, National Curricula in Mathematics, 1992).

The programme of study for Key Stage 2 lacks rigour for the most able pupils although teachers are free to teach material defined in the succeeding key stage. The programmes of study for the key stages are defined for all pupils. Topics which pupils of ordinary ability may not properly understand are placed at higher levels and do not appear in the primary programmes of study. One example is the teaching of fractions. Operations on fractions are not explicitly defined in any key stage, but are implicit in the Number and Algebra programmes in Key Stages 3 and 4. There is a good case for teaching bright pupils to handle operations on fractions and other topics, such as ratio and proportion and compound measures, in Key Stage 2. Although the content of the programmes of study is not intended to be the whole of the mathematics curriculum, in many schools that will inevitably be the case; there are few signs that teachers are prepared to teach beyond them, even for more able pupils.

Although schools have made a satisfactory start to implementing the National Curriculum for mathematics, there is a tendency for teachers to rely too heavily on published schemes. Where this is the case curriculum planning is often weak.

There is still too much emphasis on repetitive number work which does nothing to put right pupils' misunderstandings or fundamental errors. Too many pupils lack fluency in mental arithmetic and there are weaknesses in fundamental knowledge.

Insufficient opportunities are planned for pupils to apply their skills and knowledge, both in mathematics and in other subjects. There is insufficient attention paid to algebra, and data handling, in Key Stage 2.

Assessment

Schools are obliged to teach the National Curriculum programmes of study and to assess the outcomes. The attainment of pupils in mathematics is assessed according to level descriptions set out in the new National Curriculum document (*Mathematics in the National Curriculum*, DFE and HMSO, 1995). The level descriptions replace the earlier 'statements of attainment' from which they were derived and developed.

The statutory summary assessments which should be made at the end of the key stages are twofold: Teacher Assessment and Standard Assessment Tasks (SATs). Statutory Teacher Assessment should be made according to the relevant attainment target level descriptions.

The level descriptions in the National Curriculum document are intended to characterise typical pupil attainment in the attainment targets at particular levels. The attainment of primary school children is normally expected to fall within the range of levels 1-3 towards the end of Key Stage 1 (with the great majority of children attaining level 2) and levels 2-5 at Key Stage 2; again with the great majority attaining levels 4 by the end of the key stage.

A weakness of the level-related mathematics curriculum model is that there are no age-specific criteria: there is nothing specified in the attainment targets to be known and mastered at any particular age. The dependency of the curriculum and assessment of achievement on levels means that failure to learn knowledge and skills appropriate to a pupil's age can simply be accommodated by the assessment system in terms of a level and written down to ability. The system provides insufficient incentive for raising the standard of achievement of individual pupils.

It is good practice for the planning and evaluation of teaching and learning to follow a cyclical pattern. Teachers usually make weekly forecasts of their work, evaluating the learning outcomes of the class or group. This provides information which guides future work, so that the planning of lessons is strongly influenced by the school's system of assessment. This form of feedback is effective as an evaluation of the quality of teaching but assessments of individual pupils are also necessary.

The school must keep records of personal details and academic records of the achievements of individual pupils; for example, the end of key stage Teacher Assessment and SAT results. Records must be updated, annually. Records should be sent on to the next receiving school when the pupil leaves.

There is no statutory obligation for class teachers to keep formal records of the individual progress of the pupils in their class, but it would be poor practice not to do so. All that is necessary is a record of the work done by each pupil and a consistent method of recording standards achieved which will guide the teacher in making summary assessments for the annual updating of records and annual reporting to parents.

Greater attention should be paid to matching new work to prior attainment. Insufficient credit is given to what has been achieved in the previous year or key stage.

Teachers should be careful to ensure that they assess what the pupils understand, know and can do in terms of the programme of study, rather than merely making a record of what has been covered. There is no need to keep subject charts or ticklists as evidence of attainment target progress and it is unnecessary to keep folios of the work of individuals, although teachers may wish to keep key pieces of work as a reminder of individual achievement or because it is of a very high standard. Many schools keep a folio of work which exemplifies achievement at particular levels, although there is no requirement for them to do so. The School Curriculum and Assessment Authority (SCAA) produces material which exemplifies standards of work at different levels and which has been sent to schools.

It is left entirely to schools and teachers to develop appropriate ways of marking pupils' work. In Key Stage 1, much feedback to the pupil will be done immediately. Written marking gradually assumes greater importance as the pupil moves through Key Stage 2. A marking system should be consistent, so that the pupils become accustomed to the meaning of the evaluation. A good marking system should distinguish between attainment and effort. Written comments, particularly on extended pieces of work, guide the pupils and can help them to improve standards. Spelling and grammatical errors in written mathematical work should be corrected as a matter of routine.

Pupils should, from as early an age as possible, be involved in the assessment of their own learning, by the setting of personal goals appropriate to their age and maturity, which, once achieved, should be replaced by new ones.

In general, teachers do not analyse the reasons for pupils' errors sufficiently well to help them to get over their misunderstandings. Where errors are made as a result of misconceptions or a lack of understanding, the teacher should listen carefully to what the pupil says and follow the reasoning in written work. Marking which is solely evaluative does not help pupils to improve the standard of their work or to eradicate the cause of their errors. Not all pupils' errors are due to misunderstandings, of course: around half of all the errors which pupils make are unstable or inconsistent. Unstable errors are mostly due to carelessness or inattention. Teachers must be able to distinguish between careless errors and those which are more symptomatic of deep-seated difficulties which can be diagnosed and eradicated.

Parents are entitled to at least one report annually of the academic and other progress of their children. Subject commentaries in reports may be brief but should evaluate standards of achievement clearly, as well as attitudes and effort. Both strengths and weaknesses should be reported. Reports should indicate the progress that the pupil is making in relation to others in the same year, and, where there are significant differences, these should be explained. In the core subjects, aggregated levels of Teacher Assessment and SATs must each be reported at the end of the key stage.

Standards of achievement

There can be little doubt that the implementation of the National Curriculum in primary schools has produced considerable benefits and has helped to improve the quality of teaching in both key stages. The most noticeable improvements have been seen in Key Stage 1 where the programmes of study have provided a welcome clarification of what should be taught and some topics have been introduced earlier than before. New standards have been set and teachers' expectations have been raised in consequence. Although there have also been improvements in Key Stage 2, it is likely that the benefits may not appear for some time owing to the longer lead time of the introduction of the programmes of study.

The first annual review of inspections found concerns about standards of achievement in relation to the pupils' capabilities in about a third of all primary schools, with standards being lower in Key Stage 2 than in Key Stage 1. It is likely that standards have risen in Key Stage 1, at least in part because the National Curriculum has clarified what should be taught, but the gains are not being capitalised upon sufficiently in Key Stage 2. Data from inspection reports shows that mathematics is the weakest of the subjects of the curriculum in Key Stage 2 (Mathematics and Science in primary schools: a review), where standards are unsatisfactory in one third of schools.

In 1996, the review of inspection findings found that standards in mathematics give cause for concern in about ten per cent of schools in Key Stage 1 and in around 20 per cent in Key Stage 2 (*Subjects and Standards. Issues arising from findings of Ofsted inspections, 1994-95,* HMSO, 1996).

Quality of Teaching

A curriculum cannot be considered without those who are expected to teach it. The demands which the National Curriculum makes upon the subject knowledge of teachers are considerable and many lack confidence in their personal knowledge and ability to teach the range of subjects well, especially mathematics in Key Stage 2. The over-reliance upon commercial mathematics schemes tends to reflect this lack of confidence.

Fewer than four per cent of primary teachers in a sample of 285 schools which were inspected between 1982 and 1986 had a main qualification in mathematics (Aspects of Primary Education. The Teaching and Learning of Mathematics, DES, HMSO, 1989). Put another way, more than three quarters of the schools lacked a teacher with a main qualification in mathematics.

The mathematical requirements for entry to courses of initial teacher training are modest. Many intending primary teachers have no higher qualification in the subject than a GCSE grade C which can be obtained via the intermediate tier GCSE syllabus, in which there is little subject depth. Because of the narrowness of the three subject A level course, only a minority of entrants to training as primary teachers have studied mathematics beyond the age of sixteen.

The Cockcroft Report (Mathematics Counts, HMSO, London, 1982) recommended that all primary schools should appoint a curriculum co-ordinator for mathematics so that the school could make the best use of its expertise. Around two-thirds of primary schools have a mathematics co-ordinator in post but it is rare for sufficient non-contact time to be given so that co-ordinators can work with other teachers. Their potential for raising the quality of teaching throughout the school is rarely fulfiled. In the first annual review of inspections, one of the main findings was that schools that achieve good standards in mathematics are invariably well managed at the subject level but few schools give co-ordinators the necessary time to develop their important role.

More recently, Ofsted finds that 'the co-ordination of mathematics is satisfactory or better in only half of schools. In about one-fifth of schools there is a link between poor management and co-ordination and low standards' (*Subjects and Standards. Issues arising from findings of Ofsted inspections, 1994-95*, HMSO, 1996).

The capacity for local provision of training varies greatly across the country in both quality and quantity. LEA advisers organised training courses in the past but much of the time of those who are left is now taken up with inspection. The advisory teachers for mathematics who were recruited in the wake of the Cockcroft Report have done their work and gone while the capacity of the teacher training institutions to provide INSET has also declined. Primary schools have felt the loss of subject-focused advice and in-service training keenly.

In-service training could do much to improve the quality of teaching; for example in Key Stage 2 there is a clear need for teachers to take in-service courses related to the teaching of Number. It is in this area that there are most weaknesses in teaching and yet it is also the area where teachers believe that they are most effective.

Where teachers are able to attend good quality training courses there are often no opportunities given to share the benefits with their colleagues.

A varied approach to the teaching of mathematics was strongly encouraged by the Cockcroft Report (1982). The famous and enduring paragraph 243 of the report states that mathematics teaching at all levels should include opportunities for:

- exposition by the teacher
- discussion between teacher and pupils and between pupils themselves;
- appropriate practical work
- consolidation and practice of fundamental skills and routines
- problem solving, including the application of mathematics to everyday situations
- investigational work. (Mathematics Counts, para 243)

In most classrooms, the range of activities remains far too narrow. In 1996, Ofsted finds that 'the range of styles deployed with a particular class is usually very narrow. A major reason for this is inappropriate and excessive use of published schemes, particularly in Key Stage 2. This leads to a poor match of work to the full range of pupils' abilities and a lack of differentiation. Where individualised learning is used extensively, teachers too rarely intervene or discuss work with pupils unless they are stuck' (*Subjects and Standards. Issues arising from findings of Ofsted inspections, 1994-95*. HMSO, 1996).

The first annual review of inspections reports that the teaching of Number in Key Stage 2 is where most change is needed. Currently, pupils spend too much time working individually. The review suggests that different teaching techniques are needed for each of the three stages of learning facts, practising skills and developing understanding. It is particularly important that teachers place a new emphasis on the development of understanding, teaching the pupils in groups of similar ability or together with others who need similar attention.

Teachers should spend more time analysing pupils' errors with a view to improving understanding. In many cases their misunderstandings and mistakes are not diagnosed correctly so that they persist without remedy. Research has shown, nevertheless, that only around half of errors which pupils routinely make in tests and exercises are due to misunderstandings and misconceptions. As often as not pupils' errors are due to carelessness and are not persistent or significant.

In nearly all schools sufficient time is given for mathematics and number work appropriately gets the greater share. The best use is not always made of the time, however. Too long is spent rehearsing skills rather than improving understanding, with pupils working individually on repetitive exercises. In particular, teachers do not spend enough time helping pupils to remedy their errors and weaknesses.

Although practical work arises in the context of the mathematics itself, opportunities for using and applying mathematics are often presented in other subjects. Strong cross-curricular links are characteristic of the best work in mathematics, in particular with upper juniors in Key Stage 2. Inspectors reported in 1989, in a review of mathematical work in schools: '...where some of the topics and themes afforded excellent opportunities for mathematics to be used as an enabling and interpretive tool. The teachers encouraged the pupils to estimate, carry out trials and effect improvements; to generalise and discuss the validity of their generalisations.' (*Aspects of Primary Education. The Teaching and Learning of mathematics.* DES, HMSO, London, 1989)

Practical equipment is essential for the teaching of number. There are many sorts of apparatus available which enable the modelling of the number system so that the child can observe, understand and become familiar with the workings of it. All pupils need to use apparatus at some stage to solve number problems until they have a sound knowledge of number facts and an awareness of place value. Slower learners need the support of apparatus well into Years 5 and 6 or beyond, and this is entirely appropriate for them. Other children should become independent of the apparatus as soon as they have the security of sure foundations of place value and well known number facts. More than a third of schools fail to make the best use of the equipment which they have. This is due to shortcomings in the planning of lessons and also to a lack of awareness of what is available.

Although equipment is important, school inspections show that it is how it is used which counts most: 'A distinctive feature of the best work in mathematics is the way in which the teacher leads the children to an understanding of mathematical ideas from relevant practical work. The examples of effective teaching show that much depends upon the teacher's ability and skill in making the mathematical content and processes of first-hand experiences explicit to the children. No matter how good the equipment, ultimately it was the quality of the exposition and dialogue with the teacher that enabled the children to reflect upon and think through mathematical problems and ideas. This factor, more than any other marked the difference between good and mediocre work' (*Aspects of Primary Education The Teaching and Learning of Mathematics*, DES, HMSO, London, 1989).

It is a pity that schools rarely use computers to teach mathematics, even though they are present in the classroom or otherwise easily accessible, owing to a lack of awareness of the range of software available and how computers can be used.

Themes and topics

For many years a standard way of teaching in primary schools has been through a general theme, topic or project in which the subjects of the curriculum are presented. This approach provides continuity of the school day, linking the work in the curriculum as a whole, and also helps to provide the practical, problem solving approach which is so necessary in mathematics. Topic work, however, is unsatisfactory where it is undemanding in terms of subject knowledge and where the topic itself assumes greater importance than the subject programmes of study.

The following factors are associated with successful topic work:

- an agreed system of planning which is consistent and carefully structured, thus helping to ensure continuity and progression;

- a degree of co-operation in planning which provides an opportunity for teachers to share the workload and their expertise;

- a careful account is taken of the National Curriculum programmes of study; topics are usually chosen to fit National Curriculum attainment targets and programmes of study; attainment targets or aspects of attainment targets that do not fit in readily are taught separately;

- topics have a single subject bias or emphasise particular subjects;

- there is whole-school agreement about subject coverage and the balance between subjects and topics, the outcomes of which are monitored by members of the senior management team of the school;

- the planning of the subject refers to learning outcomes or objectives, activities and assessment (Appendix A, *Curriculum Organisation and Classroom Practice in Primary Schools. A follow-up Report*. HMSO, 1993).

Even where mathematics is not the main focus of a project the planning should include practice and application of the skills of numeracy, including the use of statistics and graphs, as well as number, measurement and computation. Good opportunities for practice and applications are likely to arise when the topic subject is science (number, measurement, formulae, graphs, statistics, shape); technology (number, measurement, shape, formulae, ratio and proportion); geography (number, statistics, map scales, graphs); art (symmetry, pattern, shape, ratio and proportion). Opportunities arise for exploration of mathematical contributions from other cultures, especially where the focus is history and geography.

However, insufficient opportunities are presently given for applying mathematics, especially in Key Stage 2. Ofsted finds that schools should consider ways in which pupils can 'gain experience in applying their knowledge to a range of activities' (A key issue for schools, in *Subjects and Standards. Issues for development arising from Ofsted findings of inspections*, HMSO, 1996). Significantly, insufficient use is made of pupils' knowledge of handling data attainment target in their studies, the very knowledge which is most applicable in topic work.

Working in small groups

In many primary school classes, pupils are placed in small ability groups for their work in mathematics. Where the pupils in the group are of similar ability good opportunities are presented for co-operative and collaborative work. In other subjects, groupwork is seen where pupils of widely differing abilities collaborate on a shared task, making appropriate contributions and achieving at different levels. There is no particular reason why some practical and co-operative tasks in mathematics, such as measuring or conducting surveys, cannot engage all of the pupils in a class or group.

There are occasions where children need to work on their own: when writing up or quietly reflecting and generally when the company of others would impair concentration. But, for the greater part of the time, children should work in interaction with the teacher and other children. A combination of direct teaching of the class or group and one-to-one work with individual pupils is likely to provide the most effective teaching.

The best teaching is flexible and teachers are comfortable with a range of organisational strategies and teaching techniques, and planning involves selection of the most effective form of organisation and strategy according to fitness for purpose.

A multicultural dimension

The teaching of mathematics should reflect the major contributions made to the subject by different nations throughout its history but the programmes of study for mathematics make few demands and offer little guidance. The Key Stage 2 programme of study for Shape, Space and Measures states that pupils should be given opportunities to 'consider a wide range of patterns, including some drawn from different cultural traditions.'

Mathematics is the product of a diversity of cultures and traditions; there is much potential to engage pupils in the exploration of its history and in contributions to the body of knowledge made by different nations around the world. Teachers should introduce pupils to the origins of the mathematics which they are teaching for three good reasons: firstly, because the pupils would otherwise gain an incorrect view of the subject; secondly, because interest and enjoyment can be added to the pupils' learning; thirdly, because possibilities are increased for cross-curricular work.

Clearly, topic and thematic approaches have much potential with regard to cultural issues. As an example, in a humanities-based study of the ancient civilisation of the Greeks, opportunities could be given for pupils to find out how they counted, measured and calculated in those days.

Commercially produced mathematics schemes

Ofsted made three main criticisms of mathematics in primary schools in 1994:

- foundation skills in arithmetic, especially in mental arithmetic and written calculation, which are established in primary schools, are weak;

- the dominance of commercial mathematics schemes which have 'been adopted wholesale by schools and which teachers find constraining and difficult to break free from';

- individualised learning schemes 'which place undue responsibility on pupils for controlling the pace and quality of their learning. Such schemes reduce the teacher to a classroom manager, replacing the routine of class-based drills and exercises with an alternative routine of work cards and self-testing sheets.' (*Mathematics and Science in Schools. A review.* HMSO, 1994)

Most schools buy in one or more of the commercially-produced mathematics schemes and the quality of textbooks is generally adequate. Modern schemes are not merely sets of books, but are complemented by an array of work cards, consumable workbooks and investigations. These products are carefully written to provide progression in children's learning and often include guidance for teachers, usually in the form of separate books which set out the philosophy and distinctive approach of the scheme.

Some commercial schemes contain guided exercises and practical work set out so that they can be followed by the children with only routine checking and occasional help from the teacher. If teachers lack confidence in their own ability to plan the work in mathematics such a scheme is obviously attractive to them; but it can take over so that the teacher becomes an assistant, merely administering work cards and recording pupil progress through levels and books. Where teachers lack confidence in their ability to teach the subject, they are unable to extend the content of the scheme to provide suitable opportunities and challenge, particularly for the more able pupils. Some mathematics schemes are written in such detail and complexity that they can even undermine self-confidence in a teacher's ability to plan and teach the topics directly, without recourse to a scheme.

Experienced classroom teachers often express misgivings about the over-use of commercial schemes. No scheme can substitute for a balanced approach. Especially in Year 3, and, in secondary school in Year 8, (*Aspects of Primary Education: The Teaching and Learning of Mathematics*, DES, 1989), excessive reliance upon the published schemes and too much individualised learning is associated with poorer performance and achievement than where children work in a variety of different ways. In 1993, Ofsted found, in annual report (*Mathematics: Key Stages 1, 2, 3 and 4. Fourth Year, 1992-93*) that more than one-third of classes in primary schools spent too much time on repetitive exercises as a result of following the commercial scheme too closely.

Again, in 1996, Ofsted finds that 'Curriculum planning is variable and continues to be weak where schools rely too heavily on published schemes and have not supplemented them with further guidance to teachers. This occurs most frequently in schools which have not developed an underlying framework of clear objectives for their mathematics curriculum'.

Teaching children to learn intelligently

Many children's experience of mathematics consists of applying rules in order to 'get the answer'. For example, to fix the position of a decimal point in a multiplication the rule is 'add up the total number of decimal places and put the point there'. The rule leads to success with this particular class of problem; but if the pupils are not taught to understand why rules work they must rely on remembering a different set of them to solve each and every class of problem they deal with. By contrast, a full appreciation of place value of whole numbers and decimals enables the pupil to understand the significance of multiplication and division by tens, hundreds, ... and to fix the decimal point intelligently. Intelligent learning requires very few rules and leads to gradually increasing success as the pupil internalises more and more mathematical structure. As Skemp says: 'This is a much more economical form of learning, since the number of plans which can be derived from the same knowledge structure is enormously greater than the number of rules which can be learned separately' (Richard R Skemp, *Mathematics in the Primary School*, Routledge, London, 1991).

Intelligent learning consists, Skemp says, not in the memorising of rules, but the building up of structures of knowledge from which 'a great variety of plans of action can be derived as and when required'.

Of course, it is necessary to commit some facts and definitions to memory when learning mathematics, as it is for other subjects. Nevertheless, the learner should build up a sound personal construction of mathematics which is extended by applying what is known to new situations. Pupils should learn facts, such as addition and multiplication facts, so that they can be recalled immediately when required. But the knowledge of the number facts should rest upon sound understanding and internalising of the relationships between numbers, rather than parroting tables. In this way, the learner can more easily deduce fresh number facts from those already known, and thereby to grow in understanding. For example, an understanding of inverse operations, gained in Key Stage 2, lays the foundation for understanding of further work in number and algebra; for example, for solving equations – making memorizing of easily forgotten rules, such as 'change side, change sign', and 'cross-multiply', unnecessary. Throughout this book it is assumed that children are to be taught to learn mathematics intelligently, rather than by rules, rote and habit.

PART 2
THE ATTAINMENT TARGETS

1. USING AND APPLYING MATHEMATICS

The four strands of the programmes of study of the attainment target have the same headings in each of the primary key stages. The strands are intended to be delivered largely through the work in the other attainment targets: all of the attainment targets are interdependent and there is some overlap of the programmes of study.

The first strand sets out the opportunities which the pupils should be given. The remaining three strands of Using and Applying mathematics are concerned with what pupils should be taught. They are:

Strand 2

making and monitoring decisions to solve problems;

Strand 3

developing mathematical language and forms of communication;

Strand 4

developing mathematical reasoning.

Strand 1: Opportunities

In Key Stage 1, pupils should be given opportunities to

- use and apply mathematics in practical tasks, in real life problems and within mathematics itself;

- explain their thinking to support the development of their reasoning.

In Key Stage 2, where pupils are expected to exercise a greater degree of independence in their learning, pupils are to be given opportunities to:

- use and apply mathematics in practical tasks, in real life problems and within mathematics itself (as for Key Stage 1);

- take increasing responsibility for organising and extending tasks;

- devise and refine their own ways of recording;

- ask questions and follow alternative suggestions to support the development of reasoning.

The programme of study makes clear the importance of problem solving related to everyday situations; this is of crucial importance in the solving of numerical problems. At every stage in the pupils' learning of number operations, opportunities should be planned for the application of the essential knowledge through the solving of real problems.

Schools are finding difficulty with this attainment target and the extent to which the programme of study is being implemented is variable. Ofsted reports that work in this attainment target is underdeveloped in a significant number of schools (*Subjects and Standards. Issues for school development arising from Ofsted findings of inspections, 1994-95*, HMSO, 1996). The tendency for primary schools to rely over-much on the textbook scheme to take care of the balance of the attain-ment targets can lead to inadequate opportunities for genuine use and applications of mathematical knowledge and skills. In too few schools is the work in this attainment target sufficiently well planned and integrated with the other attainment targets. Too few opportunities are given to enhance the value of topic work by applying mathematical knowledge, especially of number, measurement and data handling.

In the first annual review of Ofsted inspections it is made a key issue for schools to consider ways of raising standards in numeracy, which can be broadly defined as the ability to use and apply the knowledge and skills of mathematics (*A review of inspection findings Mathematics, 1993/94*. HMSO, London, 1995). In general, schools give inadequate opportunities for pupils to use and apply their knowledge. In schools where the planning of applied work is good, pupils are given wide and frequent opportunities to apply their mathematical knowledge and skills in support of the work in other attainment targets and in other subjects. In this way they are helped to understand and to see the relevance of what they are doing and the work is carefully planned to extend their knowledge and apply skills in appropriate situations. Where pupils are given opportunities to apply and use their mathematics in other subjects this has the beneficial effect of reinforcing and consolidating mathematical knowledge in appropriate contexts and also of enhancing the learning of the subjects of the wider curriculum.

More frequent whole class sessions, in both key stages, would present more opportunities to explore problems, to consider a variety of approaches to problem solving, for discussion and explanation. Where pupils spend too much of their time working on their own they are unlikely to receive adequate opportunity to explain their reasoning and to discuss their mathematics with other pupils and the teacher. The more able pupils, and the shy ones in particular, are denied proper opportunities where the teacher spends most time helping the least able.

Pupils should be given increased opportunities to organise and plan their work. This is particularly important with Handling Data in Key Stage 2. Again, in circumstances where pupils are working for too great a proportion of their time on the textbook scheme they are unlikely to be given the necessary experience of organising and planning their work which is called for in the programme of study.

The proper equipment should always be available: diagrams or pictures in textbooks of measuring equipment or whatever are no substitute for the real thing. The pupil should have a clear idea of what is to be done and assess what equipment is required and get it ready before beginning work.

Strand 2:

Even where pupils have a good understanding of the mechanics of a mathematical operation, such as division, and can model it with apparatus and get the right answer, it does not follow that they can translate a practical problem and select an appropriate process for solution. Practice of arithmetical procedures is important but must be kept in balance: pupils are not likely to be given sufficient opportunities to select appropriate mathematics if their mathematical diet contains too much in the way of repetitive exercises and sums. In fact, they can usually do the calculations but lack experience in solving problems in a practical context. A key task is to teach them to untangle problems which are embedded in language and to select the numerical operation appropriate to the solution of a given problem.

Application of their knowledge of measurement is important. There is a strong tradition, in Key Stage 1, of the development of measurement concepts, especially those of length, weight and capacity. The early success gained in Key Stage 1, of measuring, needs to be extended in Key Stage 2 to a wider range of standard units of length and weight and to area and volume. Much more work needs to be planned so that the pupils apply and extend their understanding of measurement and knowledge of units. Again, the tendency to rely too heavily on the textbook scheme in Key Stage 2 can lead to restricted experiences of measurement.

It is disappointing that more opportunities are not given for pupils to practice and consolidate knowledge of the Handling Data attainment target, since such work is so clearly applicable to everyday life.

The pupil should reflect on numerical results to problems and be asked about the reasonableness of the answer, exercising increasingly informed judgment in Key Stage 2, as to whether the results (of calculations, investigations or surveys) are reasonable. This is best done in a group or class discussion so that the pupils can compare their ideas with others.

Strand 3: Developing mathematical language and forms of communication.

Pupils need to learn mathematical terms and their definitions. Although they generally enjoy a reasonable degree of success with words associated with shape, such as the names of polygons, they are less successful with definitions and properties of shapes. There is a need for greater clarity which can only come through discussion and explaining to others.

There is a general lack of understanding of the language of the relationships between numbers (eg multiple, factor, divisor) throughout the key stages. Many pupils achieve poorer examination results at the end of Key Stage 4 than they should, owing to a weak grasp of the meaning of elementary mathematical terms; for example, a small group of sixth formers repeating their GCSE course in order to improve their grades in mathematics were seen to be baffled by this question in a past examination paper which they were using for practice: in the following list 'circle the numbers which are multiples of three'. Not one of these students, all seventeen years old, were able to answer this trivial question because they did not understand the meaning of the term 'multiple'.

The use of symbols is an essential part of mathematical language and communication. Just as it is necessary to select an appropriate operation and method for the solution of a problem, it is important to be able to communicate the information to others efficiently and unambiguously. Mathematical symbols are unambiguous and should be used with precision. Pupils often misinterpret the equality sign as an instruction to do something. Signs, such as those for equality and inequality, or the sign for the division operation, should be introduced carefully and rigorously.

Pupils should be taught to use a range of appropriate diagrams, tables and graphs. Graphical methods clarify the problem and improve the communication of it and its solution to others. Sketches or diagrams help to plan and organise work and often suggest a route to its conclusion. Pupils should be aware of alternative ways in which information may be presented; for example, the choice of a bar or pie chart.

They should be given opportunities to discuss the possibilities and to justify their decisions.

Strand 4: Developing mathematical reasoning

Investigating within mathematics itself provides opportunities for pupils both to develop their reasoning abilities and their understanding and knowledge of mathematics.

Opportunities should be given frequently for pupils to make and test general statements and to make predictions. 'Doubling always gives an even number', 'the numbers in the five times table always end in a zero or five' or 'cutting the corners off any polygon doubles the number of sides' are examples of general statements which can be tested. Pupils should learn that making a general statement which is true puts them in a powerful position. When they observe that adding 10 increases the number in the tens column by 1, they should be encouraged to explore the idea further until the general nature of the idea is known and understood. At that point, particular results can be predicted, based upon the generalisation; for example, that $37 + 10 = 47$.

Again, if a child understands and knows that $6 \times 7 = 42$, and has observed that reversing the numbers in multiplication does not affect the result, the child can predict that $7 \times 6 = 42$.

Increasingly, pupils should be expected to explain their thinking. Although difficult, it is essential for them to develop their capacity to organise their reasoning in words and in writing, leading eventually to using symbols and diagrams.

Teaching this strand of the attainment target is difficult, even for specialist teachers of mathematics. In many secondary schools, and in a growing proportion of primary schools, much of the time given for using and applying mathematics has been taken up with free-standing investigations. It must be pointed out that these investigations are not essential but, where planned to support new ideas, or to reinforce existing knowledge, this work can be very beneficial. It also makes easier the teaching of the reasoning strand of using and applying mathematics. Properly planned as an integrated part of the curriculum, free-standing investigations can help pupils to extend their awareness of pattern and extend their knowledge of important number properties. It also helps teachers to provide a suitable challenge to those of higher mathematical ability.

An example of a free-standing investigation is the well-known 'handshake problem' which is based on the triangle numbers. Imagine that each guest at a party shakes hands with all other guests exactly once. The problem is to discover how many handshakes are there if there are a given number (n) guests. It is easy to devise variations which are mathematically equivalent; for example, a games or sports league where each team plays all others, once.

This problem is suitable for pupils of a wide range of age and ability. When setting investigation problems of this kind, the teacher selects the number of guests (n) to suit the ability and maturity of individual pupils (with differing n for different pupils).

The objective is for pupils to learn to explore problems, organising their work and recording their findings and results systematically. Ultimately the aim is for pupils to be able to present an algebraic generalisation but only exceptional pupils are likely to attain that in Key Stage 2 and only a minority in Key Stage 3.

Most pupils will need the support of a 'structure for solution' if they are not to lose their way.

- be methodical
- make a plan and write it down
- use sketches or diagrams where they are helpful
- try simple cases first
- set out the results clearly (in a table or chart)
- look for a pattern and describe it
- draw conclusions
- make a general statement
- explain the reasoning.

Tackling the handshake problem in a methodical fashion, an average pupil might write a simple plan along the following lines. 'I will investigate the number of handshakes when there are two, three, four, five, ... guests. I will draw a diagram to make sure that I do not miss any out. I will make a table showing the results for each number of guests and I will see if there is a pattern.'

The diagrams will look something like this:

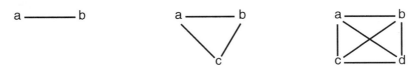

and the table like this

Number of guests	Number of handshakes
2	1
3	3
4	6
5	10

Table for the handshake problem

The majority of pupils in Year 6 should be able to organise their work along the lines indicated above. They should be able to solve the problem for a given number of guests (providing that the number is small enough for the diagram strategy to continue to work), reading their results from the table. If they can give particular solutions correctly for up to six or seven guests will have achieved appropriately for pupils of average ability for their age (level 4).

The more able pupils will spot the number pattern and be able to use it to make predictions. At that point they are likely to stop the diagram strategy and write the table by predicting and continuing the pattern

(1,3,6,10,15,21,...). If they know the set of triangle numbers they may recognise and identify them. They should be able to make an attempt at a general solution along the lines '... if there are three guests the handshake number is the second triangle number; if there are four guests the handshake number is the third triangle number...' If they can do this then they are working at a level (around level 5) which is above average for their age.

Only exceptional pupils will be able to give a general, mathematical solution to the problem which will enable the number of handshakes to be calculated for any number of guests. Such a pupil would probably not need the same degree of structure as less gifted pupils and may not need to use the same procedure (and which does not easily lead to an algebraic solution). The pupil is more likely to 'see through' the problem quickly, reasoning along these lines: 'If there are 6 guests, each guest shakes hands with five others; that is $6 \times 5 = 30$, but divide by two since we have counted them twice so there are $1/2 \times 5 \times 6 = 15$ handshakes. Generalising, if there are n guests (where n is any number), each guest shakes hands with $n - 1$ other guests. Since there are n guests, that appears to make $n(n-1)$ handshakes, but we must halve this number as otherwise we are counting them twice. The total number for n guests is, therefore, $1/2 \, n(n - 1)$.'

Having come this far the investigation can continue with the triangle numbers. It is easy to see now that the triangle numbers are equal to successive sums of the counting numbers. More precisely, the nth triangle number is equal to the sum of all counting numbers up to and including n. The first four are shown below.

$$1 \qquad\qquad = 1$$
$$1 + 2 \qquad\quad = 3$$
$$1 + 2 + 3 \qquad = 6$$
$$1 + 2 + 3 + 4 \quad = 10$$

Alternatively, they could be shown diagrammatically.

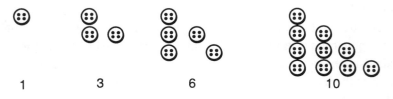

1   3   6   10

Triangle numbers.

Each of the array of buttons representing a triangle number is half of the rectangle n(n + 1). For example, the array in the diagram below shows that the fourth triangle number can be represented by half of the rectangle number 4 x 5 = 20

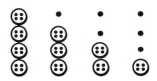

Fourth triangle number.

The fourth triangle number is, therefore, 1/2 x 4 x 5 = 10

Generalising in symbolic algebra, the nth triangle number is equal to

    1/2 n(n + 1)

The possibilities for variations on this investigation are endless, of course. That is true of many of these investigations. In fact it is unfortunate that many pupils repeat the same investigation with a succession of teachers. Putting the problem in different terms would go a long way towards eliminating the possibility of staleness and would allow pupils to build upon previous experience.

Where the teaching aims at giving a structured approach to the work in strand 4, as in the handshake problem, much of the work in this strand can be done through mathematical investigation.

2. NUMBER

The first strand of the programme of study for Number contains, as usual, the opportunities which should be given to all pupils within the key stage.

There are four remaining strands of the attainment target.

Strand 2

> Developing an understanding of place value (and, in Key Stage 2, extending the number system)

Strand 3

> Understanding relationships between numbers and developing methods of computation

Strand 4

> Solving numerical problems

Strand 5

> Classifying representing and interpreting data. (there is no fifth strand since there is a separate attainment target for Handling Data for that key stage).

Strand 1: Opportunities

In Key Stage 1, pupils should be given opportunities to:

- develop flexible methods of working with number, orally and mentally;

- encounter numbers greater than 1000;

- use a variety of practical contexts and resources;

- use calculators both as a means to explore number and as a tool for calculating with realistic data, eg *numbers with several digits*;

- record in a variety of ways, including ways that relate to their mental work;

- use computer software, including a database.

and at Key Stage 2, pupils should be given opportunities to:

- develop flexible and effective methods of computation and recording, and use them with understanding;

- use calculators, computers and a range of other resources as tools for exploring number structure and to enable work with realistic data;

- develop the skills needed for accurate and appropriate use of equipment.

In both primary key stages, schools give sufficient attention to number work, in terms of the time allocated, but the best use is not always made of it, particularly in Key Stage 2. The standards of achievement in number knowledge and skills are generally sound in Key Stage 1. Place value, however, is not tackled early enough in some schools and paper and pencil algorithms are sometimes introduced too early, before the pupils have the knowledge and recall of addition and subtraction number facts essential to do the paper and pencil work with proper understanding. The foundations for number work which are laid down in Key Stage 1 are not always built upon well enough in Key Stage 2. The rate of progress is too slow, especially where pupils are allowed to work individually, at their own pace. Too many are unable to recall the basic number facts appropriate to their age in Key Stage 2 and too much of the time devoted to mathematics is spent practising skills and routines rather than consolidating knowledge and developing understanding. Although there is a need to improve the speed and accuracy of computational skills in Key Stage 2, many pupils are prevented from doing so, and are held back, because of poor basic knowledge. More emphasis should be placed on solving numerical problems and opportunities given to ensure that the pupils know which operation is required in a given situation, develop a sound grasp of place value and a thorough recall of essential number facts, such as multiplication tables. Too many pupils lack fluency in mental arithmetic and are unable to tell whether their answers are realistic.

The National Curriculum placed a renewed emphasis upon mental arithmetic. The Cockcroft Report (*Mathematics Counts*. HMSO, 1982) drew attention to the decline in teaching of mental arithmetic in schools, finding that, in many classrooms, mental calculation had disappeared altogether owing to the spread of individualised learning and a consequent lack of emphasis on oral and aural work. Mental arithmetic is now required to be taught in both key stages, although neglected for a generation. Most teachers now in service were not taught mental methods themselves. It is not surprising that there is a general lack of confidence. Mental arithmetic is difficult to teach, not least because of the non-standard, idiosyncratic connections which the learner must make and which need time to develop. To achieve success pupils need a secure foundation in the structure of number, especially place value, number facts and an awareness of number pattern.

Nearly all schools teach their pupils to use calculators but the potential of the calculator to improve understanding of number concepts, such as place value, is rarely exploited well enough.

In general, insufficient opportunities are given for pupils to use computers to develop their work in this attainment target. In conjunction with a suitable range of software computers can be used effectively to improve the speed and accuracy in recall of basic number facts; to consolidate place value concepts, including decimals; to calculate with fractions and percentages; to develop graphical work using graph plotting software; to develop concepts in algebra, such as the order of operations, with simple spreadsheets.

Strand 2: Developing an understanding of place value and extending the number system

The training of teachers as specialists in either one of the two primary key stages can leave them with an incomplete understanding of the ways in which pupils learn mathematics, especially important concepts of number. The text of this chapter contains references to early numerical work; for example, the teaching of counting and cardinal number. Although I hope that all readers will find them useful, they are written especially for those who specialise in the teaching of Key Stage 2 classes.

The sequence of teaching and learning activities which lead to counting necessarily involves *matching*. If two sets have the same number of members, the members can be paired off or match each other. Mathematicians say that sets with the same number are *equivalent*. Typical pre-counting, matching activities are the setting out of a knife and fork (knife matches fork); shoe and glove pairs (gloves match each other, match hands); putting coats on to pegs or hangers; putting name labels on to pegs; giving out milk or equipment to each child in the class or group; putting toys and games in their special places (marked with pictures of the objects); making a display for the wall and matching children's names to the parts with which they have been directly concerned. Some of these matching activities, although planned, do not need special lesson time; they take place at other times, such as breaktime, or are part of the daily routine.

Counting is a matching activity where the number words, in order, correspond to the members of the set to be counted. The counting numbers, or natural numbers are the set of positive whole numbers: 1,2,3,... The members of any finite set are countable. The number of members of a finite set is called the cardinal number of the set: any whole number or zero. The cardinal numbers are, therefore, 0,1,2,3,... When a finite set is counted, the number words are matched off to the set of objects being counted. An infinite set (eg the set of whole numbers) cannot be counted and therefore has no cardinal number. It is a paradox that the set of counting numbers is itself uncountable. In order to count accurately, we need to know the counting numbers — at least as many as there are objects to be counted. Each counting number matches exactly one of the objects being counted, in one-to-one corres- pondence. At the end of the count, the last number gives the cardinal number of the set of objects

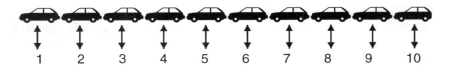

One - one correspondence

Although young children may know the number names before beginning school and may be able to recite them in the correct order, this is not necessarily counting in the true sense. A child may speak the number names, moving a finger along the objects but without the necessary precision in matching the object to the number word so that the number names bear no exact relation to the objects being counted. For a proper understanding of counting, the child must learn to:

- put the objects, physically at first, into a set for counting;

- know at least as many counting numbers as there are objects to be counted;

- know where to start the count and where to end: both the number sequence and the objects being counted;

- say the counting numbers in the correct order, without missing or repeating any of them;

- match each counting number with exactly one object, all objects being matched, physically by touching or pointing;

- give the last number in the 'count' as the size of the set;

- understand that the cardinal number remains constant unless the composition of the set is altered (conservation of number).

A characteristic property of the set of knife, fork, spoon is that the members of the set are the utensils with which we eat our food. But this set has another important property — its cardinal number. It is a member of the set of all sets which have the same cardinal number — three. We can recognise the number of small sets without needing to count the objects involved; it is second nature to recognise the sets of cardinal number two and three although we are generally unaware as to how we are able to do it. It is a skill which must be learned.

The characteristic property of the set of all sets whose cardinal number is 3, is that number itself. Similarly for 4, 5, 6, ... objects. Numbers of objects can be recognised in this way up to about six or seven, but not far beyond. It is important that pupils learn to recognise this visual property of small numbers, in order to count and to make visual estimates. Beyond the limit of six or seven, we need to re-group objects into smaller and more manageable numbers, so that eight objects can be seen as three and five, two fours, four twos, or six and two.

Younger pupils may not yet have grasped that the cardinal number of a set remains fixed and independent of the position or orientation of its members. In the recent revision, conservation of number, as it is called, has lost its place in the programme of study. It is easy to test: firstly, a pupil counts a set of objects such as beads, counters or buttons arranged in a line on a table. The objects are now moved further apart or dispersed over the surface of the table and the pupil asked whether there are now more or fewer objects than before. If the pupil has grasped that the number is independent of the length of the line (or the position of the objects on the table) he or she will give the same answer as before without the need to count again. If not then the pupil has not achieved 'conservation' of number.

The programme of study of the attainment target Using and Applying Mathematics requires that pupils should be taught to relate numerals and other symbols to a range of situations. Numerals, technically speaking, are not numbers but the symbols which represent them. Pupils are able to record single digit numerals in their mathematics if they know and can use number words and recognise numerals in everyday contexts such as bus and house numbers and games. In contrast to some other symbols, children manage to read, understand and record numerals without much trouble. Numerals are relatively free of difficulty; they are part of the familiar, everyday world. Other symbols are first met at school, such as those for operations and equality.

The counting numbers (1, 2, 3, ...) can be shown on a number line which is often a useful part of the permanent classroom display. It can be progressively extended as the children's number concepts are developed.

Zero is an early addition to the counting numbers, when the children understand the need for a zero symbol. The number line is useful for counting, for counting on from a given number, for counting back, for counting in twos, threes, fives and for ordering.

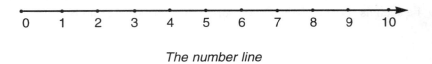

The number line

Fractions and decimals can be represented on the number line. When extended to the left, beyond zero, the number line shows negative numbers. A number line can be horizontal, or vertical, like a thermometer.

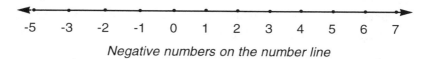

Negative numbers on the number line

Pupils must learn what is meant when we say that one number is less or greater than another. They learn to do this by comparing small sets, by matching and one-one correspondence.

The ordinal numbers (first, second, third, fourth,...) occur naturally in everyday speech.

At some stage the teacher will wish to introduce the signs

    < 'less than'

and

    > 'greater than'

in the context of ordering whole numbers, probably using the number line.

Place value

The way the Romans wrote their numerals suffered from the great disadvantage that they had no symbol for zero. Zero acts as a 'place holder' in a numeral like 340. Without a zero symbol it is difficult to distinguish between thirty four and three hundred and forty. Even so, Roman numerals are still in use, even today; examples being faces of clocks and watches and the tabulation of documents.

Our system originated in India (around 750 AD) and came to Europe via the countries which we now know as Iran and Iraq (800 AD) and Egypt (900 AD). Leonardo Fibonacci realised the significance of the numerals used in the Moslem world and introduced the system of numerals consisting of a zero and nine digits to the universities of

Europe in 1202, although they were known and in use in Moorish Spain as early as the year 970. The new system vastly improved the ability to record numbers, including fractions and decimals, but the most important feature was the ability to calculate with the numerals themselves, rather than with counters or the abacus. Although the appearance of the numerals which we inherited has changed over the centuries, both Hindi and Arabic numerals survive today in much the same form as they were at Leonardo's time.

Any number, from 2 onwards, can be the 'base' of a number system with place-value. Our number system is base 10 or 'denary', like that of the Romans. Base two (binary) requires only two digits, 0 and 1. This is the simplest system which could be devised and is associated with modern digital switching 'on/off' technology, as in computers. It was fashionable in primary schools not so long ago to teach children to work with bases other than ten, in the expectation that they would understand base ten better if place value was approached through general principles.

This strand requires that pupils should be progressively taught to read, write and order numbers up to 1000, developing an understanding that the position of a digit signifies its value.

Apparatus is necessary to do this effectively; for example, a set of 36 objects (loose, linking cubes are convenient) can be arranged as three groups of 10 and six single units, recording the number on a *place value board*.

Place value board showing the number 36

The board shown is arranged in tens and units, but will later be extended, when working with larger whole numbers to hundreds and, later still, to thousands. The great advantage of working with linking cubes is that the 'tens' can be broken down into 'units'.

Pupils should practice making up numbers on the place value board, and recording them. Some teachers like to use an intermediate form of recording known as extended notation, which has certain advantages; for example, reinforcing the idea of the special nature of the ten digit. Extended notation is not, however, essential; a disadvantage is that the pupil has to learn the usual notation later.

Working with larger numbers is best done with apparatus which models the base ten number system more conveniently than linking cubes which are really too big except with smaller numbers. It is important that the units can be bundled or exchanged to make tens and can be decomposed again into units. There are different structured materials designed for teaching place value and number operations such as Multibase, which consists of units, longs (tens), flats (hundreds) and large cubes (thousands). With this type of equipment the tens are not broken down (decomposed) into units but exchanged for them.

hundreds	tens	units

Place value board showing 235 with Multibase apparatus

An abacus also models the number system. Tens are not broken down into units nor the hundreds into tens, but can be exchanged.

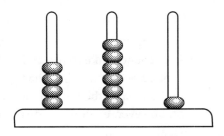

The number 461 shown with a spike abacus

In Key Stage 1, pupils solve money problems, making up small amounts of money from coins and giving change first with small sums and later to sums greater than £1. In contexts such as these, the pupils first meet and record the decimal point. Using metric units of measurement, pupils' understanding of decimals is further extended in Key Stage 2. The place value board can be used with decimal fractions in a similar way to whole numbers. A choice has to be made for the units when using the Multibase base ten equipment: using flats for units provides for two places of decimals (longs for tenths and singles for hundredths).

Some educators believe that aspects of place value such as decimal fractions should be introduced earlier in view of the routine use by children of calculators in the classroom. Calculators, although useful to make points quickly and to reinforce ideas of place value, are no substitute for structured base ten apparatus.

The following list shows the knowledge required for a true understanding of place-value with whole numbers:

- ordering numbers to at least 10, 100, 1000;

- when given a number, of two or more digits, in words, orally or in writing, to set it down in numerals, on paper or to enter it into the keyboard of a calculator; conversely, when given the numeral in digits, to be able to read it in words or write it in words on paper;

- knowing that the position of a digit indicates its value; given a number of at least two digits, to say how many units a particular digit represents; for example, in the number 365, the six represents sixty units, and the three, three hundred;

- when given a whole number such as 39999, knowing that the next number will be 40000;

- knowledge of the relative values of one place to another, and especially an appreciation of zero as a place holder; for example, that the three in 350 is ten times that of the three in 35;

- multiplying and dividing a whole number by a (positive, whole number) power of ten;

- using approximations, including significant figures.

Similarly, with decimals:

- the meaning of the decimal point in money;

- understanding remainders and knowing when to round up or down;

- given a decimal in words orally or written, to set it down in numerals, on paper or on to the keyboard of a calculator;

- using decimals in the context of measurement to two decimal places;

- calculating with decimal numbers;

- using and understanding the notation for recurring decimals and the rounding error on the calculator, 1/3 = 0.3 recurring;

- in calculations (written) involving decimals, to get the decimal point in the correct place;

- make approximations to a given number of decimal places or significant figures;

- appreciating the result of multiplying or dividing a decimal fraction by a power of ten, especially in the context of related units (for example, g and kg);

- ordering decimals, including those given to different numbers of decimal places; for example, understanding that 2.37 is less than 2.4 but greater than 2.369.

Fractions

In Key Stage 1, children bring intuitive ideas of fractions from their everyday use of words, such as half and quarter. Teaching of fractions should build upon this and develop the concept of *a whole* which can be divided into equal proportions or parts: eg two halves or four quarters. This is done in practical situations: an apple to be shared by two children; a jugful to be poured into four equal measures; lengths of string to be cut exactly in half. When children are sharing things, the idea of a 'fair share' contributes to their understanding of the equality of each half or each quarter.

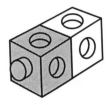

Two halves, cubes of different colours

Understanding of equivalence of fractions is not required in the Key Stage 2 Programme of Study. Pupils need to have some understanding of equivalence, nevertheless, in order to make sense of other work; for example, fractions and percentages of quantities (Strand 3). An arrangement of four Multilink cubes, two each of different colours shows two halves making the whole and that two quarters are equivalent to 1/2.

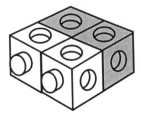

Two quarters are equivalent to one half

The understanding of the equivalence of one unit, ten tenths and one hundred hundredths should be developed in the pupils' work on decimal place value.

Strand 3: Understanding relationships between numbers and developing methods of computation.

Early algebraic ideas are intended to be developed through number. In Key Stage 1, the Programme of Study for Number includes the exploration of simple number patterns developing to the recognition of number sequences in Key Stage 2.

In Key Stage 1, patterns arise where pupils are learning addition and subtraction facts, multiples of two and three, exploration of odd and even numbers; for example, the pattern arising from finding totals to 7:

0 + 7 = 7	7 + 0 = 7
1 + 6 = 7	6 + 1 = 7
2 + 5 = 7	5 + 2 = 7
3 + 4 = 7	4 + 3 = 7

The related pattern for subtraction or difference is:

7 - 0 = 7	7 - 7 = 0
7 - 1 = 6	7 - 6 = 1
7 - 2 = 5	7 - 5 = 2
7 - 3 = 4	7 - 4 = 3

The visual patterns which the pupils would make with concrete materials helps them to remember the number facts. The written number sentences also show a variety of patterns and illustrate the *commutative* property of addition of numbers;

for example,

1 + 6 = 7   6 + 1 = 7

It is not so obvious to the learner that 3 + 4 is equivalent to

4 + 3, when using concrete materials, but it becomes apparent from the number sentences, when the pupil speaks and writes them:

6 + 3 = 9 and 3 + 6 = 9

Subtraction of numbers is not, of course, commutative; for example,

9 - 3 = 6   whilst 3 - 9 = - 6.

Divisibility

In Key Stage 1, pupils should learn to recognise numbers which are divisible by 2, 5 and 10 when learning multiplication facts. In Key Stage 2, this can be extended to divisibility by 3 and 9. Although divisibility does not appear explicitly in the revised version of the programme of study for either key stage it is implicit in the requirements for mental arithmetic.

The idea of digital root is useful for showing divisibility by 3 and is also a tool which has its uses in investigational work. The digital root of a number is obtained by summing the digits; if the number so obtained has more than one digit, the process is repeated until a single digit remains; for example, the digital root of 167 is 5.

Summing the digits of 167 we have 1+6+7 = 14.

14 has two digits so the process is repeated.

1+4 = 5, the digital root.

In the set of multiples of 3: 3, 6, 9, 12, 15, 18, 21, 24, 27, 30, 33, 36, 39,... each of the numbers 0-9 occur as the final digit, in recurring order 3, 6, 9, 2, 5, 8, 1, 4, 7, 0. The digital roots are always 3, 6 or 9 – a test of divisibility by 3.

Knowledge of divisibility by 2,3 and 5 is an important key to mental arithmetic. The knowledge can be extended. If an even number has a digital root of 3, it follows that it is divisible by 6. By investigating digital roots, pupils can deduce that the digital root of all multiples of nine is 9. This is the test for divisibility by nine.

Pattern in the 100 square

In Key Stage 2, children can explore patterns arising in the 10 x 10 multiplication square. The square is symmetrical about the *leading diagonal*, which shows the commutative property of numbers with respect to multiplication. Division of numbers, like subtraction, is not commutative of course.

Visual number patterns occurring in the 10 x 10 table square can be picked out. The multiples of four have been deleted from the square to make the pattern in the following table.

Patterns made by other multiples are worth investigating, but the square should be extended beyond 10x10.

1	2	3		5	6	7		9	10
2		6		10		14		18	
3	6	9		15	18	21		27	30
5	10	15		25	30	35		45	50
6		18		30		42		54	
7	14	21		35	42	49		63	70
9	18	27		45	54	63		81	90
10		30		50		70		90	

10x10 multiplication square, multiples of four removed.

Factors

The numbers 1,2,3,4,6,8,12 and 24 are factors of 24:

$$24 = 1 \times 24$$
$$= 2 \times 12$$
$$= 3 \times 8$$
$$= 4 \times 6$$

The number 24 is, therefore, a multiple of 8 distinct factors, 1, 2, 3, 4, 6, 8, 12, 24

Investigating some other numbers...

2 = 1 x 2 (two factors)

8 = 1 x 8, 2 x 4 (four factors)
9 = 1 x 9, 3 x 3 (three factors)
16 = 1 x 16, 2 x 8, 4 x 4 (five factors)
1 = 1 x 1 (one factor only)

All whole numbers, other than 1, have at least two distinct factors: 1 and the number itself.

A number which has more than two distinct factors is called a *composite* number, or sometimes a *rectangle number.* Rectangle numbers can be shown as rectangular arrays:

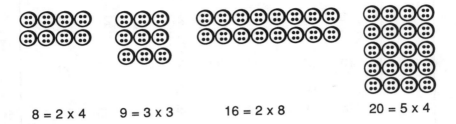

| 8 = 2 x 4 | 9 = 3 x 3 | 16 = 2 x 8 | 20 = 5 x 4 |

Rectangle numbers

Numbers which are not rectangle numbers are known as prime numbers. A prime number can be defined as one which has exactly two distinct factors — one and the number itself (by this definition 1 is not a prime number).

A prime number cannot be shown as a rectangular array.

The Sieve of Eratosthenes

The Greek philosopher and mathematician, Eratosthenes, who lived and worked in Alexandria around 230 BC and was a contemporary of Archimedes, is especially remembered for his method of finding all the prime numbers less than a given number, known as the 'sieve of Eratosthenes'.

To find all primes less than 100 using Eratosthenes' sieve, take a hundred square; we will find the primes by eliminating numbers which have fewer or more than two factors.

Firstly, eliminate the number 1, which has one factor only.

Now remove all multiples of 2 in turn except two, itself (exactly two factors).

Now eliminate all multiples of 3 (apart from 3 itself). The multiples of four have already disappeared. Repeat with multiples of five repeat until the numbers remaining are the primes less than 100.

	2	3		5		7		
11		13				17		19
		23						29
31						37		
41		43				47		49
		53						59
61						67		
71		73				77		79
		83						89
91						97		

The sieve of Eratosthenes after the third pass

Even better, this can be done in three dimensions. The number square is laid out on a 100 grid (of 2cm squares or larger). Instead of eliminating numbers, cubes are placed on the multiples. Pupils make their own decisions as to colour coding of the multiples.

Square numbers

This pattern of square numbers shows how they 'grow':

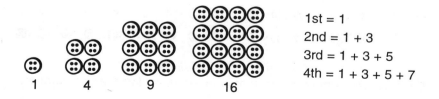

1st = 1
2nd = 1 + 3
3rd = 1 + 3 + 5
4th = 1 + 3 + 5 + 7

1   4   9   16

How square numbers grow...

Triangle numbers

The triangle numbers are also an important set of numbers. They featured in an investigation in the preceding chapter.

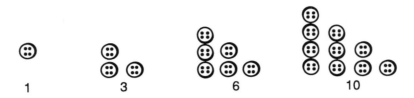

The first four triangle numbers

The pattern of buttons representing the triangle numbers shows that the numbers are equivalent to the sequence

1, 1+2, 1+2+3, 1+2+3+4, ...

The sequence continues in this way for as long as we like. The 30th triangle number, for example, is equal to the sum of all of the positive whole numbers up to 30. For a larger triangle number (the 100th, say), pupils can use the memory facility of a calculator to sum the integers to 100.

In the triangle number 'handshake' investigation, a relationship was shown between the triangle numbers and related rectangle numbers. Another interesting connection between the square and the triangle numbers can be shown by a dot array.

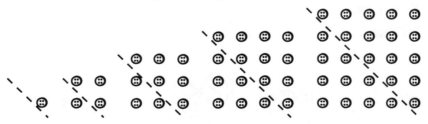

Square and triangle numbers.
Each square number is the sum of two consecutive triangle numbers.

Square roots

Just as they should know the square numbers, at least up to 100, so pupils should recall the associated square roots. Calculation of square roots of numbers other than the first ten or so perfect squares, which occur in the multiplication tables, should, of course, be done with a calculator.

Cube numbers

Naturally, the cube numbers must be shown in three dimensions. Using linking cubes the pupils will quickly run out of cubes!

They will then try drawings, models or improvise with Multibase apparatus.

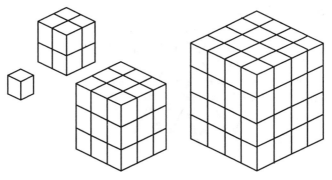

The first four cube numbers: 1, 8, 27, 64

Fibonacci Numbers

The Fibonacci sequence is generated by adding the previous two numbers to get the next one, starting the sequence with 0,1,...

0, 1, 1, 2, 3, 5, 8, 13, 21, 34, 55, 89, 144, ...

This famous and interesting number sequence takes its name from the twelfth century mathematician who was greatly interested in it. It was, however, well known to Chinese and Indian scholars many centuries before his time.

The sequence has many intriguing features; for example, the ratio of consecutive numbers becomes ever closer to the Golden Ratio. Fibonnaci numbers often occur in nature, in the structural arrangement of pine cones, sunflowers and many other plants and seeds (see, for example, Mottershead, 1990).

Finite Differences

Investigating the differences between successive terms of a sequence often enables the prediction of subsequent terms; for example, the first seven cube numbers are

> 1, 8, 27, 64, 125, 216, 343, ...

More advanced pupils can extend and explore the pattern, using a calculator. In this case, the differences of successive terms of the sequence are:

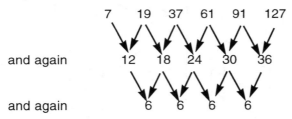

and again

and again

Working backwards, to predict the next term in the sequence of successive differences, we get $6 + 36 + 127 = 169$. The eighth cube number is, therefore, $343 + 169 = 512$. This process can be used to predict subsequent terms of a large class of sequences.

Mappings and relations

The mathematical term relation describes the way in which sets of things or (especially) numbers are connected; mapping refers to the dynamics of the relation.

> Alice, Jane, John, Mary and George are members of the same family. If their ages are known the names of the people could be linked with their ages, like this:

the age of this person is ...

Alice ⟶ 8

Jane ⟶ 10

John ⟶ 31

Mary ⟶ 35

George ⟶ 39

Mapping showing the relation
'the age of this person is.'

The relation 'the age of this person is' maps the name of the person onto their age in years.

Here is a mapping showing another relation among the members of the same family, The relation is 'is a sister of'.

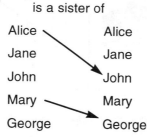

Mapping showing the relation 'is a sister of'

Again, here is the mapping 'is a child of'

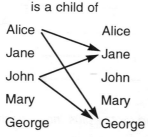

Mapping showing the relation 'is a child of.'

Although now removed from the programme of study by the latest curriculum review, the idea of a 'relation machine', which models a mapping, has certain advantages which may ensure its survival. Using 'machines' helps pupils to explore what happens in a mapping and helps the teacher to introduce or reinforce algebraic ideas, such as inverse operations, inverse elements and the introduction of use of letters-for-numbers symbolic algebra.

The illustration shows a machine which adds three to any number 'input' together with its mapping diagram. The 'output' number which emerges on turning the handle is three more than the input.

The plus thee relation machine

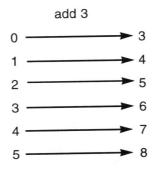

Mapping for the plus three machine

Pupils can make their own machines and devise mechanical internal workings if the teacher wishes. The machine can be made reversible, illustrating that addition and subtraction are inverse operations.

Doubler machine.

This machine is a 'doubler', a times two machine: it generates the 2-table. When reversed, the doubler becomes a 'halver' machine, re-inforcing the ideas of inverse operations for multiplication and division.

Halver machine

The halver divides by 2. Using both doubler and halver machines together shows multiplication and division as inverse operations.

Flow diagrams

A flow diagram of a relation is a similar idea to the machine. It can also help teaching about inverse operations and for introducing symbolic algebra.

Here is a flow diagram for a 'plus four' relation: it adds four to any number which is entered.

input ⟶ $\boxed{+4}$ ⟶ output

The reverse flow diagram shows that subtracting four 'undoes' the effect of adding four — and vice versa. Similarly, dividing by four undoes the effect of multiplying by four -and vice versa.

output ⟵ $\boxed{-4}$ ⟵ input

Symbols and formulae

In Key Stage 2, pupils should be taught to express simple formulae in words, and later, to use algebraic symbols. They need to learn the conventions.

In the case of the plus four relation, we say that whatever number the input may be, the output is that number plus four. This generalisation is symbolised as $y = x + 4$

$$x \qquad\qquad x + 4$$

input ⟶ $\boxed{+4}$ ⟶ output y

$$y = x + 4$$

any number, symbolised by a letter, conventionally x, entered into the function results in an output of $x + 4$. The output is symbolised by a letter, y, so that $y = x + 4$

The output, y, depends upon the value of the input, x. y is called the dependent variable and x the independent variable.

Priority of operations

The convention in arithmetic is that the operations multiplication and division take priority over addition and subtraction.

Multiplication takes priority over subtraction, so 6 x 5 - 3 means 'six multiplied by five, three subtracted from the result', it does not mean 'six multiplied by the difference of five and three'. If we wish to write 'six multiplied by the difference of five and three' in symbols, we must use brackets: $6 \times (5 - 3)$

Brackets take priority over operations, which means that we must deal with the content of the brackets before doing anything else.

The two functions $y = 2x + 3$ and $y = 2(x + 3)$ mean quite different things. The flow diagrams should make things clear:

$y = 2x + 3$

x · · · · · · · · · 2x · · · · · · · · · 2x + 3

input $\longrightarrow$ [x2] $\longrightarrow$ [+3] $\longrightarrow$ output y

$y = 2x + 3$

example: if $x = 2$, $y = 7$

$y = 2(x + 3)$

x · · · · · · · · · x + 3 · · · · · · · · · 2(x + 3)

input x $\longrightarrow$ [+3] $\longrightarrow$ [x2] $\longrightarrow$ output y

$y = 2(x + 3)$

example: if $x = 2$, $y = 10$.

Coordinates in the first quadrant

The number line is a set of points which represents numbers in one dimension — a straight line. Two number lines intersecting at right angles make the familiar x-axis, y-axis grid or *Cartesian plane*. The location of any point in the plane can be indicated by a dot. The point location is conventionally written as an ordered pair of numbers, the co-ordinates of the point, which represent the numbers of units from the origin in each of the directions of the x and y axes, respectively; for example, the co-ordinates (2,3) refer to the point located at 2 units on the x axis, and 3 on the y.

The x and y axes intersect at right angles at the point (0,0), called the *origin*. The axes divide the plane into four quadrants. The use of all but the first of these requires an understanding of negative numbers and their relation to the positive numbers, as shown on the number line.

Although extension of the plane into four quadrants is a feature of the programme of study for Key Stage 3, it can provide a good context for the application and use of negative numbers, where pupils have been taught to understand them, along the lines indicated, in Key Stage 2.

There are many children's games which are useful for practising the use of co-ordinates. They are usually based upon maps and are given names like 'Pirate's Treasure' or 'Flint's Gold'. Note that some of the games work with addresses (squares like a city A-Z map or as in the game of battleships and cruisers) rather than point 'locations'.

In Key Stage 2, pupils should be taught to understand ordered pairs as representing point locations in the first quadrant and that sets of points which define a shape such as a quadrilateral (defined by the co-ordinates of its vertices) and lines which represent the relationships between numbers such as, for example, multiplication tables.

The four operations of number

The four operations, addition, subtraction, multiplication and division are each appropriate in the solution of a variety of problems. Multi-plication is applicable in the following situations, for example.

1) Three children have five books each; how many altogether? (three sets of five: 5 x 3)

2) John has three times as many sweets as Mary, who has two. How many has John got? (multiplying factor; 2 x 3)

3) George works 45 hours at £8 per hour. How much does he get? (rate; £8 x 45)

It is as important to know which procedure to use in the solution of a problem — whether to add, subtract, multiply or divide — as it is to be able to perform the operation. Pupils learn the skills of choosing the appropriate operation, sometimes called a 'translation' of the number problem, by practising problem solving in context. There is no other way of doing it.

Although number work is usually done with an adequate support of practical equipment in Key Stage 1, the tradition of a structured approach in Key Stage 2 is less strong. Apparatus for the teaching of number operations is not always used sufficiently well to achieve true understanding in Key Stage 2, where there is a tendency for pupils to be introduced to written algorithms too early.

The word algorithm is derived from the name of the mathematician Al Khwarizmi. An algorithm, such as the familiar procedure for long multiplication, is a procedure or series of steps for carrying out calculations. In the National Curriculum there are no particular algorithms specified to be taught or known. There are at least two standard algorithms for subtraction and, apart from the more familiar one, there is a choice of algorithms for multiplication; for example, the following which is based upon repeated addition, the method of 'doubling'.

Calculating 356 x 9:

$$356 \times 1 = 356 \text{ *}$$

doubling $\quad$ $356 \times 2 = 712$

again $\quad$ $356 \times 4 = 1424$

and again $\quad$ $356 \times 8 = 2848 \text{ *}$

$$\text{* } 1 + 8 = 9$$
$$356 \times 9 = 356 + 2848$$
$$= 2904$$

Multiplying by two digits is just as easy.

To calculate 25 x 37,

$$37 \times 1 = 37 \text{ *}$$

doubling, $\quad$ $37 \times 2 = 74$

again $\quad$ $37 \times 4 = 148$

and again $\quad$ $37 \times 8 = 296 \text{ *}$

and again $\quad$ $37 \times 16 = 592 \text{ *}$

$$\text{* } 16 + 8 + 1 = 25$$

therefore, $25 \times 37 = 592 + 296 + 37 = 925$

This algorithm for multiplication works just as well as the traditional one and it is easier to understand. Although there is plenty of mental addition and estimation involved it does not give as much practice in rehearsal of the multiplication facts as the more traditional algorithm. Doubling works in reverse for division.

Towards the end of Key Stage 2, higher attaining pupils should be able to divide a three-digit number by a two-digit number. For example, to find 481/23 the procedure is much like multiplication:

```
                 23 x 1 = 23
doubling   23 x 2 = 46
again         23 x 4 = 92 *
and again 23 x 8 = 184
and again 23 x 16 = 368 *
* 92 + 368 = 460      23 x 4 and 23 x 16
                              23 x 20 = 460 (as close to 481 as
                              we can get)
481/23      = 4 + 16 Remainder 21
                = 20 21/23
```

In Key Stage 1, most effort should be spent on achieving mental fluency and recall of number facts, including sums, to ten and then beyond, and related differences, applying the knowledge gained to solve problems. The programme of study also includes the multiplication and division facts associated with the two, five and ten tables. Pupils should be taught to develop a variety of methods for finding sums and differences of number pairs, including 'using the fact that subtraction is the inverse of addition'. With numbers beyond ten, pupils use apparatus to model numbers with a growing understanding of place value; there is little to be gained by teaching written algorithms at this stage.

Learning addition facts

The aim is for the pupil to learn and know all the addition facts, firstly up to five, then to ten and thereafter to twenty and beyond. It is usual for pupils to be taught to make up given numbers with apparatus; for example, a set of five objects can be partitioned in two subsets in the following ways:

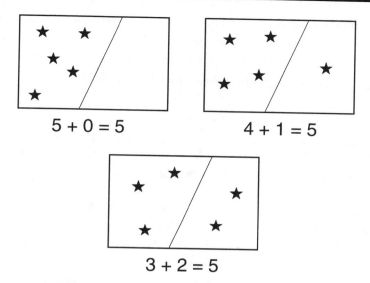

$5 + 0 = 5$ $4 + 1 = 5$

$3 + 2 = 5$

This also models the related subtractions; for example, the partition of the set into one plus four or four plus one models the two subtractions five minus one equals four and five minus four equals one. No harm is done by leaving the subtraction to later when the addition facts are becoming well established, if the teacher prefers, but recording of the number sentences in words and written symbols should accompany the modelling with the apparatus.

A 'number tree' showing five minus three.

After a time the patterns of the bonds and the associated addition (and subtraction) sentences become known and can be recalled at will. When the pupil does not need to count, the facts are truly known.

Addition facts can be reinforced by means of the number line.

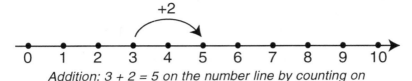

Addition: 3 + 2 = 5 on the number line by counting on

At this stage, number problems are about the apparatus itself (buttons, blocks, etc) which is being used, but later the apparatus will be used to model problems embedded in language such as 'two people are in a room and three come in. How many are there now?'

The number facts are extended beyond ten, to twenty. When these are known, the pupil has a sound basis for the number patterns beyond; for example,

$$4 + 7 = 11$$
$$24 + 7 = 31$$
$$34 + 7 = 41$$

the calculator is a useful aid in developing the pupils' awareness of the patterns.

The number line can be used to show subtraction as counting back, in a similar way to counting on with addition.

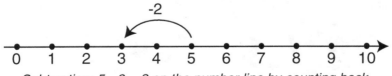

Subtraction: 5 - 2 = 3 on the number line by counting back

An understanding of negative numbers is expected in Key Stage 1. It is difficult to think of many contexts in which negative numbers arise in everyday life; examples are temperature, tidal markings and Plimsoll lines (indicating loading levels of ships). But abstract mathematical contexts are many and varied; for example, the calculator display and, later on in Key Stage 2, graphical work can be extended to four quadrants if the teacher wishes. The number line should be extended to show negative numbers.

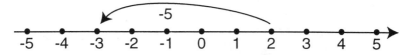

Subtraction: 2 - 5 = -3 on the number line by counting back

Difference

We need to be aware of two distinct aspects of number which are modelled by the operation of subtraction: 'taking away' and 'comparison' or difference. Matching and comparing two sets we can find the 'difference' in number. What is the difference in the numbers of pencils?

John's pencils
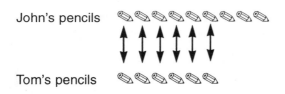
Tom's pencils

Comparison: difference of 9 and 6 is 3

Multiplication

In Key Stage 1, the programme of study requires that pupils should be taught the multiplication and associated division facts in the two, five and ten times tables. The mathematical convention is that the first number of a product is operated upon by the second; for example, 2 x 3 means 'two multiplied by three'. However, the products 2 x 3 and 3 x 2 are equivalent, because multiplication is commutative, as we shall see. It is usual to teach multiplication; for example, 2 x 3, as three sets of two.

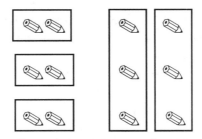

The products 2 x 3 and 3 x 2

In Key Stage 2,pupils are specifically required to be taught to understand multiplication as repeated addition; for example, that four sets of three are numerically equal to 3 + 3 + 3 + 3.

Although 4 x 3 (three sets of four or 4 + 4 + 4) and 3 x 4 (four sets of three or 3 + 3 + 3 + 3) are equivalent they are not the same.

Products can be explored as arrays; containers with convenient arrays of cells such as bun trays, egg boxes and trays, peg boards, milk crates and large sheets of squared paper marked in squares are all useful.

Objects can be placed in the cells to model simple problems such as 'three cars with two people in each, how many people altogether

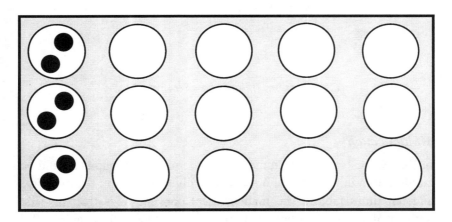

2 x 3 = 6. Bun tray representing three sets of two

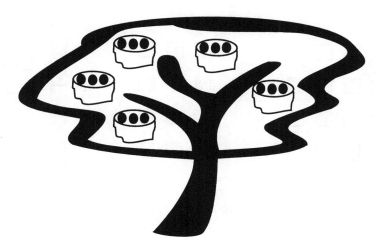

*A number tree showing five nests with three
eggs in a nest (3 x 5)*

Using the number line with products of small numbers helps to
reinforce the idea of multiplication as repeated addition.

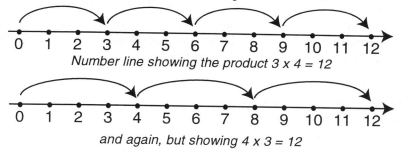

Number line showing the product 3 x 4 = 12

and again, but showing 4 x 3 = 12

Standard base ten equipment comprises 1 cm cubes which are used as
units, 10cm lengths which represent tens, 10 cm squares which represent hundreds and 10 cm cubes which represent thousands. The equipment is too small for little hands in early number work but comes into
its own for the teaching of place value and for solving number problems.

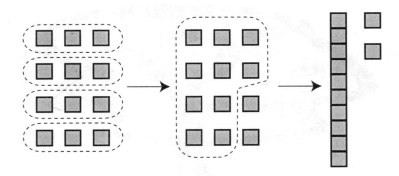

3 x 4 with base ten materials

Pupils should begin to commit the multiples in the multiplication tables to memory as early as possible, i.e. as soon as they understand products and can use apparatus to solve multiplication problems. The multiples of two, five and ten give little trouble; pupils are required to be taught them in Key Stage 1.

Allowing for the commutative property of multiplication, if pupils know the two, five and ten times tables as required in the programme of study for Key Stage 1, the following nineteen multiples remain to be learned to complete the Key Stage 2 target:

3 x 4
3 x 6   4 x 6   6 x 6
3 x 7   4 x 7   6 x 7   7 x 7
3 x 8   4 x 8   6 x 8   7 x 8   8 x 8
3 x 9   4 x 9   6 x 9   7 x 9   8 x 9   9 x 9

The first ten square numbers can be learned as a special set in the work on number pattern. This would then leave:

3 x 4
3 x 6   4 x 6
3 x 7   4 x 7   6 x 7
3 x 8   4 x 8   6 x 8   7 x 8
3 x 9   4 x 9   6 x 9   7 x 9   6 x 9

The nine times table is not difficult to learn: the first ten multiples are

09, 18, 27, 36, 45, 54, 63, 72, 81, 90

The first zero has been added to make the symmetry of the number pattern more complete. If the pupils can manage those without too much difficulty, they are left with:

3 x 4
3 x 6   4 x 6
3 x 7   4 x 7   6 x 7
3 x 8   4 x 8   6 x 8   7 x 8

The remaining three multiples of three give little trouble.

Now only the awkward squad remains, but there are only 7 of them.

4 x 6
4 x 7   6 x 7
4 x 8   6 x 8   7 x 8

Aspects of division

In Key Stage 1, pupils are taught division as *sharing* and *repeated subtraction*. Learning the multiplication facts in the two, five and ten times tables will enable them to link the operations when they are solving number problems. At this stage, however, even if they know some multiplication facts, most children are only beginning to be aware of multiplication and division as inverse operations. It is therefore essential that they have access to materials which model the division problems on which they are working. Using concrete materials, they can deal with remainders in solving practical problems.

The Key Stage programme of study repeats that pupils should be taught the two aspects of division: sharing and repeated subtraction. The repeated subtraction aspect is sometimes called 'grouping' or 'quotition'; the two aspects of division are explained in more detail in the following text. Throughout this key stage, pupils are extending their knowledge of number facts and consolidating their understanding of the operations multiplication and division as inverse of each other. Children should gradually become independent of concrete materials through the key stage, as they develop their capacity to use mental and written methods for solving number problems.

1. *Division as **sharing**, without **remainder***

Twenty sweets are shared equally by four children. How many does each receive?

The set of 20 is partitioned in 4 equal subsets. The size of the set and the number of subsets are known *but the size of each of the subsets is to be found.* We are sharing the 20 objects by 4, distributing the members of the set into the four subsets.

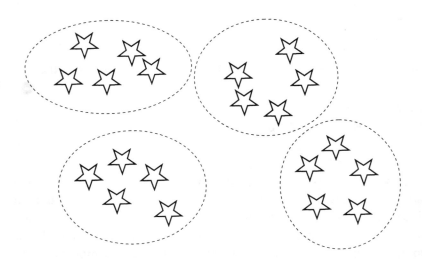

20 shared by 4 = 5

2. *Division as repeated subtraction, without remainder*

Twenty four eggs are to be packaged in boxes of six. How many boxes are filled? Children use egg boxes and convenient small objects to represent eggs.

In the case of repeated subtraction, the size of the set and of each of the equal subsets (the number repeatedly subtracted) are known *but the number of subsets must be found.* This is done by partitioning in subsets of six, i.e. six is repeatedly subtracted. Four subtractions exhausts the set.

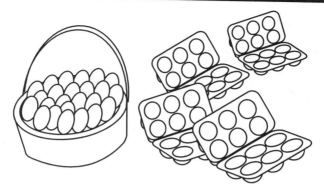

Repeated subtraction of six from 24, which fill four boxes
24 ÷ 6 = 4 exactly.

Repeated subtraction can be shown on the number line in a similar way
to repeated addition, as below

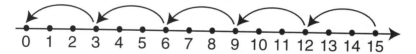

Repeated subtraction (dividing) on the number line
showing 15 ÷ 3 = 5. 3 is subtracted 5 times.
There is no remainder

Division with remainder

1. *Division as* **sharing***, with* **remainder***.*

Twenty-one sweets are to be shared by four children. How many do
they each receive?

Sharing twenty-one objects in four equal whole number subsets cannot
be done. There are four subsets of five and a remainder of one.

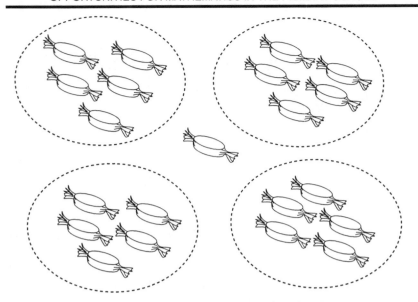

Sharing with remainder each child has five sweets.
One remains, when they are shared
21 ÷ 4 = 5, remainder 1.

2. *Division as repeated subtraction, with remainder*

Problem: Twenty five eggs are to be put in boxes of six. How many boxes are filled? Equal subtractions of six from a set of twenty five objects leaves a remainder of one. In this case the remainder is a fraction of a box: 1/6.

Repeated subtraction with remainder
$25 \div 4^{1}/_{6}$

Percentages

Percentages are ratios which, like fractions, arise in common usage in shopping, school and at home. In Key Stage 2, pupils should learn the equivalence of common percentages such as 50%, 10%, 25%, with the fractions 1/2, 1/10, 1/4; to understand that percentages are convenient ways of expressing ratios in a standard way, 'per hundred'. They should become familiar with describing proportions of quantities in terms of percentages and using them to make comparisons; for example, 45% of the infants, but 65% of the juniors live more than one mile distant from school.

Pupils should be taught to make calculations of percentages of quantities in context, especially of money and measurement, using a calculator where appropriate.

Operations on negative numbers

Pupils must be taught to extend methods of computation to add and subtract negative numbers are introduced. Negative numbers in realistic contexts such as temperature, bank balances and tide tables. If the outside thermometer records a temperature of 4^0 Celsius a fall of 6^0 results in a temperature of -2^0. If the temperature now rises from 2^0 to 8^0, the rise in temperature is 10^0. This is best done with a number line.

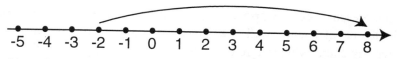

Negative numbers on the number line: rise in temperature of 10^0.

It is not necessary for teachers to take this topic far beyond the ideas illustrated in the following example. Nevertheless, the teacher may wish to extend the work for more able pupils to include graphical work in the four quadrants (as in the programme of study for Key Stage 3). The pupils should have a good understanding of negative numbers as numbers in their own right before attempting this. This should be gained through working with the number line and with exploration of of addition and subtraction of negative numbers using a calculator (N.B. some simple four-function machines which are otherwise suitable, cannot deal with signed numbers).

Using calculators

The Cockcroft Report supported the idea that calculators should be used in both primary and secondary school classrooms, whilst drawing attention to the need for training which new technology had brought. The National Curriculum has settled the arguments as to whether pupils should be taught to use calculators in primary schools or not, since that is now required; but a sensible balance should be struck between mental, paper-and-pencil arithmetic and the calculator in routine work. Inspectors reported that, in the best schools, which strategy was used was a matter of choice: 'Children accustomed to using mental arithmetic, pencil-and-paper methods and calculators generally made sensible decisions about which to use. Where calculators had been properly assimilated into the work of the school they offered much more than the means to carry out difficult computations or checking answers obtained by other methods. They stimulated fresh ideas and new thinking, helped the pupils to appreciate number relationships and contributed to the children's understanding of place value and decimal fractions.' (*Aspects of Primary Education The Teaching and Learning of Mathematics*. HMSO, 1989)

At the present time, few primary schools are exploiting the potential of calculators sufficiently well to enhance the quality of pupils' work, in either key stage. Much more than merely a calculating tool which replaces slower methods of computation, the calculator can make a significant contribution to learning by making exploration more immediate, especially in open-ended situations and number investigations, and can enable children to tackle a much wider range of tasks. A practical problem or investigation often involves large numbers which are too big or awkward for pupils to deal with by paper-and-pencil methods. Investigation of number patterns and sequences by paper and pencil methods is too cumbersome and slow.

The calculator makes a wider range of mathematics accessible to pupils and can help to teach number concepts; for example, inverse operations and the ideas of the number operations of multiplication and division as repeated addition and subtraction. The requirement to teach pupils to multiply and divide by powers of ten, (such as 10, 100, 1000), where the numbers to be multiplied or divided give rise to whole number solutions is best met through work with the calculator.

Strand 4: Solving Numerical Problems.

This strand of Number links with and supports the programme of study for Using and Applying Mathematics and there is a considerable overlap of the two attainment targets.

Difficulties arise for pupils when solving numerical problems in selecting the operation to use — addition, subtraction, multiplication or division: the *translation* of the problem. They need plenty of practice. A pupil who has been thoroughly drilled in computational skills may be quite unable to apply his or her skills to solve practical problems in context. The experience of many children with 'sums', is still too abstract, lacking a practical context.

Estimation

Estimation is relatively new in the mathematical curriculum.

One type of estimate is a sort of quantity surveying; for example, to find roughly the number of bricks needed to build a wall. The number of bricks to the square metre could be calculated, or the number in a course and by extension, the number needed for the whole wall.

Estimates involving measurement are usually given in standard units. To give an accurate estimate of the distance from where we stand to a given point when giving directions; to make a good guess about how long it would take to complete a certain task; to judge that the height of a door is about two metres: all of these are skills of estimation which are essential in everyday life. These skills are dependent upon a confident and accurate appreciation and feel for standard units.

Estimation sometimes involves comparison; for example, in estimating the height of a tall building a pupil could compare its height with that of a person standing close to it.

It is wise to make an estimate before using a calculator and to check that the answer arrived at is reasonable. As an example, if 48 is multiplied by 72 we should expect an answer to be around 3500 (50 x 70). A calculator display of 3456 is close to the estimate but if the display were 34560 the discrepancy would indicate that an error had been made. Pupils should be taught the skills of estimation of the size of expected answers to problems and to check their results systematically.

Approximation

When making calculations we should give the answer to a problem only to the degree of accuracy which the situation demands; for example, if the result of the calculation of the area of a school hall gives the result 406m^2, it makes sense to round the answer down to the nearest hundred. In Key Stage 2, pupils should be taught to round numbers up or down to the nearest ten or hundred.

Using the calculator presents the need to round decimals. This should generally be appropriate to the units of measurement which the pupils handle routinely and which arise in the context of money problems, i.e. no more than two places of decimals.

Strand 5 (Key Stage 1 only)

Classifying, Representing and Interpreting data

The fifth strand of the programme of study for Key Stage 1 contains two main elements:

- sorting and classifying;
- data collection and processing.

Sorting and Classifying

The pupils should learn to sort and classify objects against clear criteria, such as their physical properties.

For many years, sorting activities have been tools for the development of concepts and language, particularly, but not exclusively, in mathematics. Typically, pupils sort or compare objects against criteria such as size, shape, weight or number; for example, a Year 1 pupil might engage in sorting of 'heavy' and 'light' objects, comparing them, talking about them and refining the understanding of the words and the concepts.

A group of pupils is discussing plane shapes. One attribute is the number of sides. The pupils sort and classify the shapes according to the criterion 'quadrilateral', on a board.

Having sorted the set the pupils should be given the opportunity to explain their reasoning and take the activity further; for example, sorting the quadrilaterals according to a new criterion, 'rectangle'.

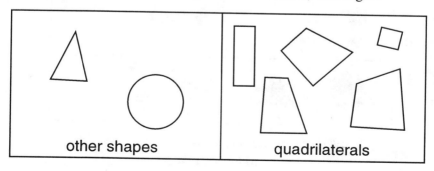

| other shapes | quadrilaterals |

Sorting plane shapes

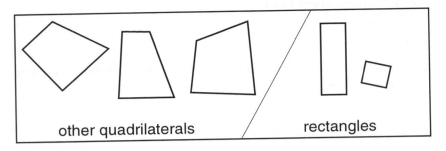

other quadrilaterals   rectangles

Sorting of quadrilaterals into rectangles and other quadrilaterals

Extending the process of classification further: the rectangles can be sorted into squares and other rectangles. Note that a rectangle which is not a square is called an oblong, a term which is correct but rarely used these days.

Pupils can use a variety of graphs and diagrams in their work on sorting; for example, Venn and Carroll diagrams, mappings and tree diagrams.

As part of a project on the environment, a class is making a collection of leaves. They classify the leaves using two attributes: size and texture. The size criteria are 'big' and 'small', those for texture are 'shiny' and 'rough'. They make a Carroll diagram and mount their leaves on it, according to the criteria.

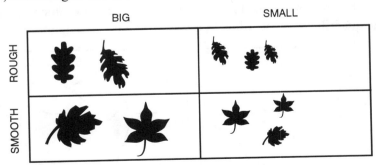

Carroll diagram showing leaves classified according to two criteria.

Imagine that a survey about pets is being done by a class. The pupils' pets include dogs, cats, rabbits and goldfish. Some of these animals are carnivorous and others are not. Some can swim, yet others cannot. Appropriate diagrams can help to clarify the criteria and help pupils to come to conclusions.

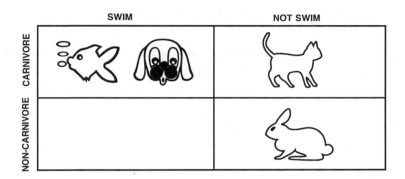

Classification using a Carroll diagram.

Another way of illustrating the information is with a 'tree diagram'.

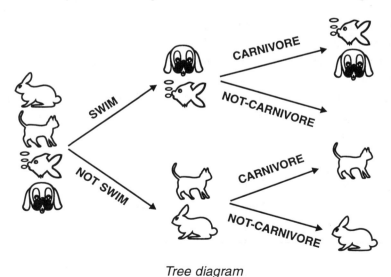

Tree diagram

Collection and processing of data

Collection of data and its analysis should be purposeful i.e. it should be done to answer a question; for example, what pet animals do the pupils keep? Are boys are heavier than girls? How many of the children who walk to school are under eight years of age? With younger pupils, the subject of an enquiry is likely to be initiated by the teacher, but nevertheless in discussion with them. Topics should be chosen so that data is readily accessible.

Data can be collected on a prepared data sheet, which must be simple and designed to obtain the right information.

Having collected the data it can be set out in a table or on a database.

OUR PETS

Animal	Names
Dog	Ruff, Jess, Lad, Ben
Cat	Blackie, Whisky, Alice, Tiger, Spike
Rabbit	Silky, Rocky
Goldfish	Thunderbird 1, Thunderbird 2

Data collection sheet, Our Pets

A block diagram is an effective method for illustrating the data. One block represents a single animal. The blocks can be counted from the graph to show that there are four dogs, five cats and two each or rabbits and goldfish. Other arrangements are equally effective. Multilink cubes could be used to make a solid 'graph' as an alternative. The pupils could also make drawings of the animals or their names and use them instead of blocks.

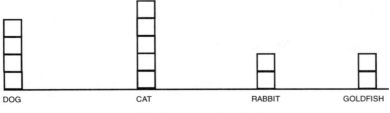

DOG   CAT   RABBIT   GOLDFISH

Block graph; Our Pets

3. SHAPE, SPACE and MEASURES

The first strand of the attainment target sets out the opportunities to be given in each key stage. The remaining three strands are:

Strand 2

Understanding and using properties of shape

Strand 3

Understanding and using properties of position and movement

Strand 4

Understanding and using measures.

Strand 1: Opportunities

In Key Stage 1, pupils should be given opportunities to:

- gain a wide range of practical experience using a variety of materials
- use IT devices, eg *programmable toys, turtle graphics packages*
- use purposeful contexts for measuring.

In Key Stage 2, pupils should be given opportunities to:

- use geometrical properties and relationships in the solution of problems
- extend their practical experience using a wide range of materials
- use computers to create and transform shapes
- consider a wide range of patterns, including some drawn from different cultural traditions;
- apply their measuring skills in a range of purposeful contexts.

Where schools plan their work well there is a good balance of the attainment targets. In these schools a good beginning has been made with the teaching of shape and space. Pupils in many schools are given good opportunities for practical work in Shape and Space although there is some neglect of practical measurement, too few opportunities are given for pupils to explore pattern, such as tesselations, and more work is necessary with computers.

In both key stages, pupils should be given more opportunities to use computer software in their work in Shape and Space. The work presently being done in schools in Key Stage 1 with programmable toys is generally good. Pupils learn to control the robot and write simple programs developing a sound foundation of understanding of rotation and angle. In Key Stage 2, the work commonly includes LOGO, or one of the varieties of Turtle Graphics derived from it. The introductory work is often good, especially where the teacher has taken a short in-service training course. Typically, the pupils learn to move the turtle around the screen and to write simple programs. When done well this links well with, and extends, that done in Key Stage 1. In general, however, the work with LOGO is not taken far enough; (this is also the case in Key Stage 3). The potential of LOGO to develop knowledge and understanding in Shape and Space is considerable. The ability to generate images of geometrical shapes helps pupils to explore reflective and rotational symmetry, to learn about angle (including estimation and measurement in degrees) and to transform plane shapes. Teaching pupils to use LOGO well is not easy. To be successful the teacher needs give time and energy to mastering it, to studying and evaluating its potential and to plan for its application in the scheme of work so that it supports and extends the work in the attainment target as a whole.

Strand 2: Understanding and Using Properties of shape.

It is intended that pupils should develop a growing awareness of the properties of common solids and polygons and their mathematical names towards the end of Key Stage 1. Young pupils should be taught to classify shapes according to simple attributes such as 'straight' or 'round'. More criteria are gradually introduced, such as the numbers of sides and vertices. Pupils make and draw them, being introduced progressively to the proper mathematical names for shapes such as hexagon and tetrahedron. This is extended through Key Stage 2 where complex properties of shapes, such as symmetry and tesselation, are explored and discussed.

Classification of shapes should involve sorting activities and discussions. It is a pity that mathematical dictionaries are rarely to be seen in classrooms; they are very useful and can help to settle points which arise in discussions. In Key Stage 2, it becomes increasingly important to teach the pupils the inclusive nature of shape; for example, that all squares are rectangles and that all rectangles are quadrilaterals.

Drawing shapes from direct observation and from imagination and making models are important for the development of the pupils' capacity to visualise in two and three dimensions. They should be given many opportunities in both key stages for practical work which involves drawing plane and making solid shapes.

Pupils can use LOGO to draw plane shapes. LOGO accepts angle inputs in degrees; although this can be modified.

More advanced pupils can programme the screen turtle to draw polygons. A knowledge of the angle properties of polygons is necessary to do this successfully.

Regular Shapes

A polygon is *regular* if its sides are of equal length and its internal angles are equal. The number of lines of reflective symmetry of a regular polygon are equal to the number of its order of rotational symmetry; for example, a square has four lines of reflective symmetry and order four rotational symmetry.

Regular Solids

The faces of a *regular* solid are congruent, regular polygons. Although there is an infinitely great variety of solid shapes, there are just five regular solids: the regular tetrahedron, the cube and the regular octahedron, dodecahedron and icosahedron, having four, six, twelve and twenty faces. These are called the Platonic solids.

The tetrahedron, octahedron and icosahedron each have congruent equilateral triangular faces; those of the cube are square, while the faces of the dodecahedron are regular pentagons.

Construction of polyhedra can be accomplished by older pupils using plasticine, pipe cleaners or commercially made kits of plastic parts (which are expensive and deny the children the valuable experience of measuring and making). Perhaps the most satisfying material — although quite difficult to work with — is stiff card, allowing for tabs which can be glued or clipped with rubber bands or paperclips (see Brian Bolt's excellent 'Mathematical Activities', containing details for making a most useful 'polyhedron construction kit').

If we take a hollow solid shape, such as a cube, and open it out flat, we get something like this:

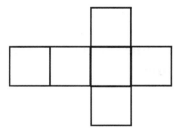

A net of a cube

This is called the *net of a cube*. It is an arrangement of six squares, called a hexomino (domino – two squares, hexomino – six squares). There are a number of different ways of opening out the cube, producing a set of different cubic nets.

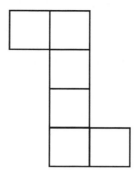

Net of cube

Doing the same thing with a regular tetrahedron produces a another set of nets. Note that each triangle of the net must connect to at least one other by an edge. Arrangements which cannot be folded without cutting or tearing in any way must be excluded. How many different nets of a cube and of a tetrahedron are there?

The Swiss mathematician, Leonard Euler (1707-1783) discovered that if the faces, vertices and edges of a solid are counted they will be found to satisfy the relation

$F + V = E + 2$

Where F = number of faces, E of edges and V of vertices.

A table showing the relation (known as Euler's relation for solids), such as the incomplete one below, can be investigated by more advanced pupils in Key Stage 2.

Name of shape	Faces	Vertices	Edges
tetrahedron	4	4	6
pentahedron	5		
cube	6	8	12
heptahedron	7		
octahedron	8		

Similarity and Congruence

In mathematics, the word similar, as applied to shape, has a special meaning which differs from its use in ordinary, everyday speech. We could say that a bicycle and a hot air balloon are similar, both being means of transport. In mathematical language, when we say that two polygons are similar we mean that they have exactly the same shape, although their sizes may differ.

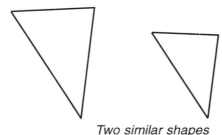

Two similar shapes

If two shapes are similar, but different sizes, one is an enlargement of the other. Additionally, if similar shapes are also the same size, they are said to be congruent.

Reflective Symmetry

Pupils in Key Stage 1 learn to recognise simple reflective (or bilateral) symmetry. A plane shape possesses reflective symmetry if there is an exact correspondence of all points and parts of the shape about a *line of symmetry* or 'mirror line'. Similarly, a solid shape has reflective symmetry if the points correspond about a plane of symmetry. A plane shape can have any number of lines of symmetry. Similarly, a solid can have any number of *planes* of symmetry.

Reflective Symmetry

The ideas of symmetry should be introduced with everyday objects and through the pupils' work in drawing, making printed patterns and observing symmetry in nature and the environment. Physical objects are generally three-dimensional rather than two, but silhouettes of objects such as butterflies and trees are plane shapes. Later, in Key Stage 2, pupils recognise the reflective symmetry of solid objects.

In Key Stage 2, pupils recognise reflective symmetry in more abstract, geometrical shapes. Mirrors, preferably the safe plastic sort, should be available for them to test geometrical plane shapes for reflective symmetry. It is difficult to see the symmetry of solid objects from two-dimensional representations so that illustrations in books are of limited use. They should be able to handle the solid objects directly, where possible and discuss them and share ideas with others. Planes of symmetry cannot be tested with mirrors, although plasticine models or other soft objects such as apples or soap can be cut in two halves about a plane of symmetry. Visualising the planes of symmetry, even of a cuboid, is quite difficult.

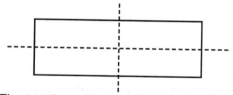

The two lines of symmetry of a rectangle.

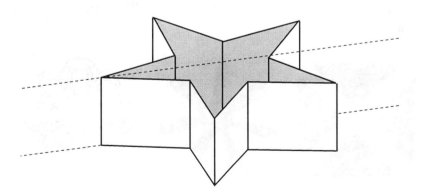

A pastry cutter has a number of planes of symmetry of which one is indicated.

Rotational Symmetry

A plane shape possesses rotational symmetry if it *maps onto itself* when rotated about a fixed point, the *centre of symmetry*. In a similar way a solid has rotational symmetry if it maps onto itself when rotated about a line, usually called the *axis of symmetry.*

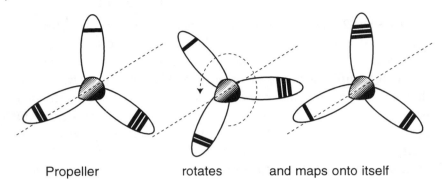

Propeller	rotates	and maps onto itself

Rotational symmetry. In a full 360⁰ rotation the propeller maps onto itself three times. It possess rotational symmetry order 3.

The *order of rotational symmetry* is given by the number of times the shape maps onto itself during a single complete revolution of 360 degrees. For example, a rectangle has order 2 rotational symmetry whilst the propeller in the above illustration is of order 3.

Using LOGO, pupils can design plane shapes with a given order of rotational symmetry.

Objects having rotational symmetry of order 4, 7, 8

Strand 3: Understanding and Using Properties of Position and Movement

1. Translation

An object is *translated* when it moves in a straight line without turning.

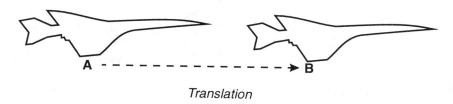

Translation

The aeroplane is translated in the direction of, and through a distance equal to, AB.

Using LOGO, the screen turtle is translated forward or backwards using the appropriate commands. Pupils can write short programs to translate pre-defined shapes about the screen.

2. Reflection.

In Key Stage 2, pupils reflect plane shapes in a mirror line. Line segments joining points and images are perpendicularly bisected by the mirror line. Note that the *sense* of the figure is changed under the reflection.

The object figure is the quadrilateral ABCD (anticlockwise). The image under the reflection is then quadrilateral $A^1 B^1 C^1 D^1$ (anticlockwise). The sense or 'handedness' has changed.

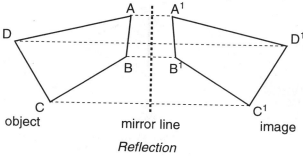

object   mirror line   image

Reflection

Points on the mirror line are unchanged by reflection: they are *invariant*.

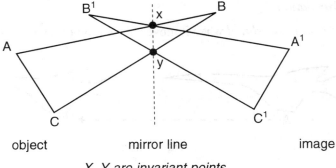

object	mirror line	image

X, Y are invariant points

3. Rotation and Angle

Teachers should be aware of the static and dynamic aspects of the angle. The static aspect is evident in 'corners' or vertices of polygons. The other aspect is apparent in 'turning' or rotation; for example, in P.E., when working with turtle graphics, the movement of clock hands or wheels. Exploring motion with programmable toys such as Roamers and generating shapes with LOGO provides pupils with suitable opportunities to understand rotation.

When a plane shape is rotated, all points, save one, move. The fixed , invariant point is called the centre of rotation. The centre of rotation is the only point which remains unchanged by the rotation.

The following LOGO program defines a simple flag shape which is useful for demonstrating rotation and translation. The LOGO commands are usually abbreviated but are left in full here.

```
forward 70
left 60
back 40
left 60
forward 40
left 60
forward 30
right 180
```

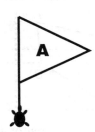

Flag shape

The flag shape was then rotated through an angle of 60⁰ anticlockwise using the LOGO procedure below. The centre of rotation is the HOME position of the screen turtle.

Program: repeat 2 [forward 70 left 60 back 40 left 60 forward 40 left 60 forward 30 right 120]

If the rotation procedure is repeated three times it will generate a pattern which has rotational symmetry of Order 6, program: repeat 3[repeat 2 [forward 70 left 60 back 40 left 60 forward 40 left 60 forward 30 right 120]]

The two components of a rotation are the direction and the amount of the turn. Although all points turn through the same angle the distance moved by each point depends upon its distance from the centre of rotation.

Using LOGO, commands to the screen turtle are given in degrees left and degrees right. This appears to cause no significant difficulty for younger pupils. That there are 360⁰ at a point or in a full turn is one of the legacies of the Babylonians, owing to the special number system, based on 60, which they reserved for astronomy and science. In Key Stage 2, pupils begin to measure angles in degrees. LOGO helps to develop a good foundation for angular measurement in degrees; for example, by estimating angles. The traditional semicircular protractor is a difficult instrument for children; circular ones or the more modern angle finders are better value for money and easier to use.

Creating Pattern from Simple Transformations

The fitting together of one or more congruent shapes without gaps in a repeated pattern is called a tesselation.

A honeycomb: tesselation of regular hexagons

In a tesselation of polygons, a number of the polygons fit exactly, with no gaps, at each vertex. If a *regular* polygon tesselates, its internal angle must be a factor of 360. Investigation will show that there are only three possible candidates: the equilateral triangle, the square and the hexagon. These are, therefore, the only regular tesselating polygons.

It is possible to make irregular polygons tesselate where regular ones would not; for example, a regular pentagon does not tesselate but the illustration below shows a tesselation of an irregular pentagon.

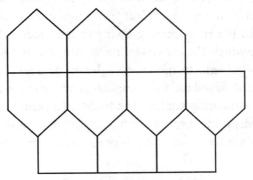

A tesselation of an irregular pentagon

Tesselating arrangements of more than a single shape are possible; for example, the tesselation of regular octagons and squares below.

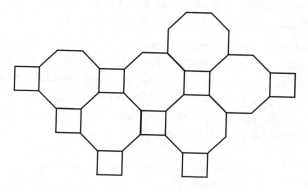

A Tesselation of Octagons and Squares

Polyominoes

A polyomino is an edge-to-edge tiling arrangement of squares, like a net of a cube. A monomino is a single square; a domino — two squares; tromino — three; tetromino — four; pentomino — five; hexomino — six squares, and so on. Cubic nets are all hexominoes.

How many distinct dominoes are there? Only one. How many distinct trominoes are there? At least two:

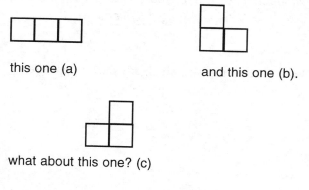

this one (a)

and this one (b).

what about this one? (c)

Polyominoes

A distinct polyomino is one which cannot be produced from a rotation or reflection of another. Each of the trominoes b and c may be rotated or reflected to produce the other are so are not distinct. There are, therefore, only two distinct trominoes: shapes a and b.

On investigating further, there are five distinct *tetrominoes*. It is easy enough to find these and to be sure that there are no more. The tetrominoes comprise 20 squares in all, but it is not possible to arrange them in the form of a 4 x 5 rectangle. However, they will make a 5 x 5 square, if a single pentomino is included. There are several possibilities, one of which is shown below.

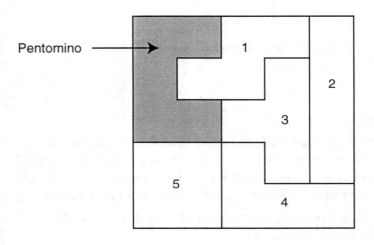

The five tetrominoes (numbered 1-5) and a single pentomino (shaded) tiling a 5x5 square.

There are twelve pentominoes, which are shown opposite.

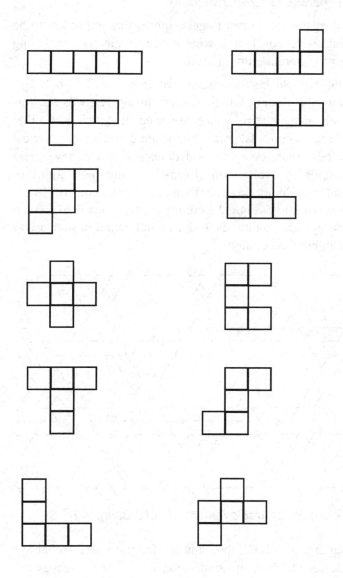

The twelve distinct pentominoes

Pattern from Different Cultural Traditions

The first strand of the attainment target requires that pupils are to be given opportunities to consider a wide range of patterns including some drawn from different cultural traditions.

Suitable examples could be the rangoli patterns with which Indian families decorate the floors of their houses during festivals such as Diwali or the abstract patterns which are used in Arabic and other Islamic art and architecture. Islamic patterns are based on geometrical shape such as hexagons, octagons and dodecagons and have great potential for pupils to explore transformations and tesselations of shapes. The reader could not do better than to acquire a copy of *Arabic Geometrical Pattern and Design*, J Bourgoin, 1973. This is in print at the time of writing this book and is designed and bound in such a way that its pages can be photocopied.

An example of Arabic Pattern, (from J Bourgoin)

Dating from around 500 B.C., the Chinese Tangram was probably a game or puzzle for children. It usually consists of seven shapes (although there is also a fifteen shape variation) which, when put together in a certain way, form a square as shown in the diagram. Work with tangram generates discussion of plane shape and helps visualisation.

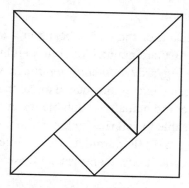

A seven-piece Tangram square

Although the pieces are few in number — a square, three different sizes of isosceles right angled triangle and a parallelogram — the possibilities for creative work in abstract geometrical figures or depicting animals, people and objects are endless. One interesting feature is the very distinctive oriental character of the shapes and patterns which emerge. For an explanation of its history and examples of its possibilities, see one of the many books on the subject; for example, Joost Elffers' book *Tangram* (1981).

Tangram figures

There are only two rules: all seven pieces should be used every time and they must be put together flat.

Strand 3 Measurement

The coins in my pocket, or the coffee beans in a jar are examples of *discrete quantities*: they are countable. Your weight, or the amount of water contained in a jug, are *continuous quantities*, which are uncountable. There are the usual exceptions which prove the rule: the grains of rice in a 500g packet are actually countable, even though it would be hopelessly impracticable to sell rice by the number of grains. It is convenient to treat rice, and other similar commodities such as sugar or sand, as if they are continuous quantities, so these substances are sold by weight.

Although continuous quantities are uncountable, they can generally be measured as long as it is practicable to do so. Measurement of a continuous quantity, such as mass or length, is always to some extent inexact and involves approximation. When reading a dial or scale the object to be measured (as with a ruler) or the pointer (as with kitchen or bathroom scales) is usually between divisions so that a decision must be made about which division on the scale is closest.

Pupils should be taught to read simple measuring equipment, such as rulers, carefully. Some children are confused about the position of the zero mark on the ruler; one type, designed for use with younger children, uses the edge as the zero mark, whilst the more usual sort has the zero a little displaced from the edge.

There is a strong tradition of measurement of length, capacity, mass and time in Years 1 and 2 and the programme of study for Key Stage 1 includes work on these measures. There is also an established tradition of the teaching of area in Key Stage 1, but no mention of area appears in the key stage programme. Nevertheless, some teachers continue to teach area to provide a firm foundation for the work in mensuration in Key Stage 2. An outline of a suitable progression of area spanning the two key stages is included in the text, later.

Pupils firstly compare and order objects, without measuring in units. Measurement involves comparison: in the case of length, objects are compared one against the other. The language of comparison and size is important. Comparing the length or the height or width of objects, they use appropriate comparatives and superlatives: same; big; bigger;

biggest; long; longer; longest; short; shorter; shortest; tall; taller; tallest;...

The distinction between mass and weight should be made here. Mass is the quantity of matter which an object contains. Weight is the heaviness of the object: the attractive force which exists between the Earth and the object, due to gravity. The force depends on the mass of the object, and on gravity. Gravity varies and is dependent on how close the object is to the Earth. Far away in space, the object would have little weight.

In the case of weight, pupils compare different objects directly, by feel. They make judgments and statements such as 'this is heavier than that', 'they are the same', 'that is lighter'. Comparing the weights of three objects in order to find the heaviest involves two comparisons.

Moving beyond direct comparison, towards units, discussion with pupils involves the questions 'how long?', 'how heavy?' 'how much?'. Initially, pupils use suitable everyday objects as non-standard units such as steps, 'feet', handspans, when measuring length. In the case of capacity they use such things as yogurt cartons or jugs. Objects can be weighed against Mutilink cubes or conkers. Improvised measures have the advantage that they can be chosen for the convenience of children to handle, are ready to hand and are independent of place-value or decimals. Improvised measures are often used in everyday life. As examples, we measure the length of a garage using our own feet or the length of the garden in paces, the flour for the cake in scoopfuls, sand and cement by the shovel.

The stage of improvised units is the time to introduce part-units; for example, 'half-steps' and 'half-cups'. At this stage, it is important that pupils appreciate that the number of units needed to define a quantity depends not only upon the magnitude of the quantity but also upon the size of the units used; for example, when measuring the capacity of a bucket in milk bottles, a greater number would be needed than would be if a larger unit, say a water-jug, were used. Two children measuring the length of the school hall choose to measure in 'steps' or 'feet'. If they choose feet, the number of units will be greater than if they had chosen steps. And if one step equals two feet, then twice as many units will be recorded.

At every stage, but particularly during the stage of learning to use standard units, the teacher should encourage the pupils to make an estimate. Estimation depends upon a thorough knowledge and feel for the size of the units; for example, they should know what a length of 25 cm looks like. At present, pupils are less at home with standard units than they should be. Where the pupils' work is dictated by textbooks there is a tendency for them to experience only a narrow range of measurement tasks and many are given too few opportunities for practical measurement of length, beyond what could be done with the standard 30 cm school ruler.

Pupils should be taught why there is a need for a standard unit. They are ready when they understand and appreciate the need to communicate to others in a standard form. In Key Stage 1, the range of standard units should include metre and half-metre, kilogram and half-kilogram, litre and half-litre, day, hour, half-hour, minute. Using litres and half-litres, kilograms and half-kilograms should be a natural progression from the improvised measures.

In Key Stage 2, pupils should be introduced progressively to a full range of metric units and be taught to convert between units towards the end of the key stage when they have a more complete understanding of place value, multiples of ten and decimals.

For many years, schools were teaching the metric system while industry and commerce still clung to Imperial measurement. Over more than thirty years, progress has been made to the point where metric measures are now the rule rather than the exception beyond school. Some Imperial units still remain in daily use and, although they are gradually disappearing, there is still a case for pupils to learn them and this is required in Key Stage 2. Those which are still useful are pounds and quarters, pints, inches, feet, yards and miles. The children should also be taught the rough metric equivalents of the Imperial units remaining in use. Routine calculations should, however, be restricted to metric units, involving imperial units only where there is a good practical reason for doing so (for example, comparing costings of floor covering where one supplier tenders in square metres and another in square yards).

In industry, although metric measures are now the rule, it is perhaps a surprise that the standard units of length are metres and millimetres. Decimetres (100mm) are almost unknown in industry, and even centimetres (10mm) are falling into disuse.

Throughout history, systems of measurement have constantly undergone change and refinement. It is interesting to note that we owe our system of measuring time — sixty seconds in a minute, sixty minutes in an hour — to the people of ancient Mesopotamia, the land between the Tigris and Euphrates, which is modern day Iraq. Two distinct number systems were used by these people: a denary system for everyday usage, and from which our own is descended, and another, highly sophisticated system based on 60 which they used for technical and scientific measurement, for example, time (the lunar calendar is 360 days), and the related astronomical and navigational angular measure (360 degrees in a circle), from which we derive measurement of latitude and longitude. The history of measurement can serve as a joint mathematics-history project which may interest older pupils in which they trace the development of the modern metric system from ancient and obsolete units such as cubits, spans, yards, feet (the king's foot), leagues, grains, ounces, pounds, and so forth.

Pupils should be taught the language of time and chronological ordering in Key Stage 1. They should understand that time can be measured and observe that clock hands move. Work could include the use of an egg timer or mechanical kitchen timer in practical situations. By the end of the key stage, pupils should understand and use standard units such as day, hour, half-hour, minute and be learning to make estimates of the time taken to complete familiar tasks. Around the end of the key stage most pupils are learning to tell the time and recognise 'o'clock' 'half-past' 'quarter-to'. In Key Stage 2, both digital and analogue readouts should be taught. The analogue clockface is an awkward device, but more analogue clocks and watches are made than digital ones, simply because people prefer them.

Mensuration: area and volume

Pupils' work should include a progression of ideas in the measurement of areas and volumes. The work should lead to a calculation of areas and volumes of plane and solid shapes, known as mensuration. Mensuration could be developed across the key stages, progressing along the lines of the following sequence.

- Direct comparison of areas of shapes: pupils discuss what is meant by bigger, smaller

- The pupils cover flat surfaces with shapes such as counters, leaves or handprints. The whole surface is covered although there may be gaps due to the shape chosen. The term 'area' is introduced. Pupils begin to make estimates of shapes where the number of units is manageable

- pupils are led, in discussion, to decide that there should be no gaps between the shapes; i.e. the shape should tesselate

- Pupils discuss the problem of communication of the area measure to others and decide that a common 'standard' shape, or unit, is necessary, such as a postcard. It should be noted that this step is common to the progression in the measurement of length, mass and capacity, as well

- Pupils measure more accurately, in part-units; For example, in halves and quarters

- Pupils measure surfaces of shapes drawn on squared paper or beneath transparent grids of squares

- The grids are now of standard unit squares; that is, the grid is marked in centimetre squares. Pupils use the grids to count squares and part squares to estimate the area of plane shapes.

- Pupils measure the perimeters of various objects and of plane shapes on a grid

- Pupils deduce the general perimeter of a rectangle

- Pupils calculate the areas of rectangles, and shapes which can be dissected into rectangles, from given dimensions, giving answers in standard units; for example, square centimetres

- The distinction is made between centimetre squares and square centimetres.
- Pupils know the formulae for the area of a rectangle and deduce those for other shapes, such as triangles, parallelograms, trapeziums, by dissection of shapes based on rectangles.
- Pupils investigate the volume of solids such as cubes and cuboids.
- Pupils extend their knowledge of algebra, deducing general formulae for areas of triangles and parallelograms and for volumes of cubes and cuboids.

Parts of the Circle, Circumference

The Key Stage 2 programme includes the practical measurement of the circumference of a circle.

A circle is the set of all points in a plane which are at a fixed distance (the radius) from a fixed point (the centre). A line segment which joins two points on a circumference is called a chord. A chord which passes through the centre of the circle is a diameter, equal in length to twice the radius.

Two diameters intersect at the centre of the circle. This property enables the centre of a circle to be found by folding or drawing.

The relationship between the diameter, d, and circumference, c, of a circle is constant; that is, the same for any circle.

$$c = \pi d$$

The number, which is represented by the Greek letter π, is an *irrational* number. An irrational cannot be expressed exactly as a fraction or a decimal but only approximated. Approximations to π are 3, 3.14 and 22/7.

The relationship between circumference and diameter can be explored by measuring the circumference, directly, with a tape measure on relatively large, circular objects, such as bicycle wheels or drums, and indirectly, by means of string; for example, on smaller objects. They should deduce that the circumference is about three times the diameter. It is important that children be given the experience of 'discovering' the relationship.

4. DATA HANDLING

The programme of study for handling data in Key Stage 1 is contained within Number, strand 5.

As always, the first strand of the programme of study sets out the opportunities which are to be given. The two further strands of the attainment target are:

Strand 2

Collecting, representing and interpreting data

Strand 3

Using and understanding probability.

Strand 1. Opportunities

Pupils in Key Stage 2 should be given opportunities to:

* formulate questions about an issue of their choice and consider them using statistical methods;

* access and collect data through undertaking purposeful enquiries;

* use computers as a source of interesting data, and as a tool for representing data.

For many schools, the National Curriculum has provided a welcome clarification of what should be taught in statistics and probability, despite recent changes and revisions. In some schools, as yet a minority, the work done in statistics is good, particularly where it supports science, history and geography, and is applied in practical situations, such as purposeful enquiries and surveys. Overall, however, the work in this attainment target remains underdeveloped, especially where it is restricted to following instructions in the textbook scheme.

The programme of study states that pupils should formulate questions about issues of their choice. Issues may emerge as a result of initial thinking by pupils but are just as likely to have been anticipated by the teacher, particularly with planned cross-curricular topics. It is important, however, that pupils are allowed to discuss the issues to be investigated in class and groups so that they understand the purpose of the enquiry fully. Statistical work, in particular, lends itself well to a cross-curricular approach. Most teachers appreciate the help of a good source book which will help to generate ideas, such as Paul Harling's book *100s of Ideas for Primary Maths* (1991).

Computer software applications, such as databases and desktop publishing, have great potential in this attainment target but are not yet exploited enough in Key Stage 2.

Strand 2, Collecting, Representing and Interpreting Data

Although sorting and classifying activities are required in the programme of study for Key Stage 1, there is no explicit mention of sorting in the Handling Data attainment target for Key Stage 2. Sorting activities are, nevertheless, quite appropriate in Key Stage 2; for example, when developing the understanding and use of properties of shape. Sorting activities are not necessarily restricted to work with concrete objects which can be seen and handled. For older pupils sorting can be both reflective and abstract; for example, to describe a set of quadrilaterals with exactly two lines of reflective symmetry is essentially a 'sorting' problem.

Pupils should be taught to interpret tables used in everyday life. There is no shortage of of tabulated data for pupils to work with. The Yellow Pages directories, train timetables, holiday catalogues, manufacturers' product and price lists are good examples of plentiful sources of tabulated data which can be used to give opportunities for sorting and classifying. The numerical information gleaned from tables can be applied in statistical work, such as average journey times, median prices and temperature ranges. Pupils should use a variety of methods to collect real data: extracting data from lists and tables; direct observation (such as monitoring traffic passing the school); using questionnaires (where information is obtained from a respondent).

Pupils should be given opportunities to plan statistical experiments and to design data sheets or questionnaires.

Statistical surveys present good opportunities for pupils to work co-operatively. The purpose of the enquiry should be clear to the pupils at the outset so that they ask the right questions and obtain relevant information.

Having collected the data, the next stage is to process it. This involves at least one of the following:

- organising the data (counting, approximating, ordering, rounding, counting, grouping)
- presenting the data in the form of a table
- entering the data into a database
- calculation of relevant statistics; for example, mean, mode, median and range
- presentation in the form of a graph, chart or diagram.

Pupils should exercise an increasing degree of independence in the planning of the enquiry as they progress through the key stage.

The programme of study states that pupils should be taught to use ... graphs and diagrams including block graphs, pictograms and line graphs... The term block graph is often used in a loose sense to mean any chart or graph which is composed of unit blocks, generally where the blocks of the graph (or actual blocks such as linking cubes) represent a single unit or a simple multiple of units. The blocks are usually drawn with spaces between them.

Block graphs are often used to represent non-numerical data such as the variety of pets the pupils keep or the different types of building in a street. In the simplest block graph, the vertical axis needs no scale. An example is given (see page 80) in Strand 5 of the Number attainment target of a block graph appropriate in Key Stage 1.

In Key Stage 2, the pupils extend the scope of the work with block graphs, begun in Key Stage 1. As part of a neighbourhood project a group of pupils survey the types of buildings in the street where the school is situated. This is a short but busy urban street. There is a mixture of housing: semi-detached, detached and terraced and a short parade of shops on one side of the street, directly opposite the school entrance, and two filling stations, one at each end. The pupils make maps and scale models of the street, and make a tally chart or frequency table to collect the data.

building	tally	frequency
Detached	卌I	4
Semi	卌卌 IIII	14
Terraced	卌卌 II	12
Bungalow	II	2
Shop	卌 I	6
Garage	II	2
School	I	1
Total		41

Frequency Table, Buildings in our Street

Pupils decide to illustrate the data with a block graph.

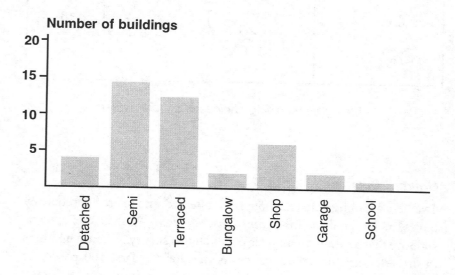

Block graph showing buildings in our street

The work done here illustrates the usage of buildings in the street but also could lead further to a survey of the shops in the parade, classifying them by the sort of goods they sell. The pupils could use a questionnaire to carry out a survey of shoppers to find the number visiting each shop and the average amount spent, illustrating the information in tables and graphically.

A form of statistical diagram which is specified in the programme of study is the pictogram or pictograph. Imagine that a group of children makes a study of the main choices of hot meals made by the 29 pupils in a class who have dinner at school. The results are recorded on a tally sheet and illustrated with a pictogram, as below. The symbol chosen represents a number of units; in this case five children.

Dinner choice	⚇ = 5 children	number
fish fingers		10
chicken		13
pizza		6

Pictogram showing choices of school dinner

Grouped Data

Teachers are obliged to teach pupils to interpret and to create frequency tables, including those for *grouped discrete data*. As an example, let us suppose that a group of pupils is conducting a survey of house numbers (a discrete variable); they decide to question the first 100 people to pass the school gate, to collect the information, recording it on a tally chart, grouping the numbers in tens, as shown.

House Number	Tally	Frequency. (Number of houses
1 - 10	̶1̶1̶1̶1̶ ̶1̶1̶1̶1̶ 11	12
11 - 20	̶1̶1̶1̶1̶ ̶1̶1̶1̶1̶ 111	13
21 - 30	̶1̶1̶1̶1̶ ̶1̶1̶1̶1̶ ̶1̶1̶1̶1̶ 1	16
31 - 40	̶1̶1̶1̶1̶ ̶1̶1̶1̶1̶ ̶1̶1̶1̶1̶	15
41 - 50	̶1̶1̶1̶1̶ ̶1̶1̶1̶1̶ ̶1̶1̶1̶1̶ 1	16
51 - 60	̶1̶1̶1̶1̶ ̶1̶1̶1̶1̶ 11	12
61 - 70	̶1̶1̶1̶1̶ 11	7
71 - 80	̶1̶1̶1̶1̶	5
81 - 90	11	2
91 - 100	11	2

Frequency table showing grouped data (house numbers)

The grouped frequency distribution can be illustrated with a frequency diagram.

Frequency (No of houses)

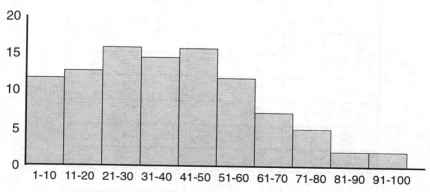

Frequency diagram showing house numbers of 100 children, grouped data.

The distinction between discrete and continuous data has arisen elsewhere in this book: discrete quantities can be counted, whereas continuous quantities are measured. The numbers obtained when tossing a die (1, 2, 3, 4, 5 or 6), shoe sizes, the amounts of money three people have on them (£0.45, £25.56, £3.67), the number of people in the bus queue, are all examples of discrete data. Examples of measured (continuous) data are timespan, the length of a piece of string, weight.

Grouping measured data involves making decisions about the boundaries of the groups (or classes), which is beyond the scope of the work for most children in Key Stage 2. The grouping of continuous quantities is not included in the programme of study. However, if measurements are rounded to whole units, the data can be handled in the same way as discrete data and can be grouped without difficulty. In the following example, the heights of children have been measured and rounded to the nearest centimetre.

Heights of 35 children (in cm)

134, 145, 148, 141, 151, 154, 143, 153, 161, 156, 156, 137, 146, 147, 153, 163, 133, 152, 153, 146, 154, 156, 147, 148, 152, 130, 147, 145, 154, 146, 152, 137, 151, 152, 144.

Grouping the data in five centimetre intervals produces the following frequency distribution.

Heights of children (cm)	tally	frequency. (Number of children)
130 - 134	II	2
135 - 139	III	3
140 - 144	III	3
145 - 149	ЖЖ	10
150 - 154	ЖЖ II	12
155 - 159	III	3
160 - 164	II	2

Frequency table, grouped data, heights of 35 children.

This data is now illustrated with a frequency chart or diagram. It is important that the class intervals are of equal width. The height of the bar is proportional to the frequency; there should be no spaces between the bars of the chart. The class intervals should be shown on the horizontal axis of the graph. This is correct but has the disadvantage that the axis appears cluttered. An alternative method is to show the lower boundaries of the intervals only, as in the graph below. If this method is chosen, it should be made clear what the block represents; for example, the first block represents the number of children who are 130cm but under 135cm tall (130cm-134-cm inclusive).

Frequency(No of children)

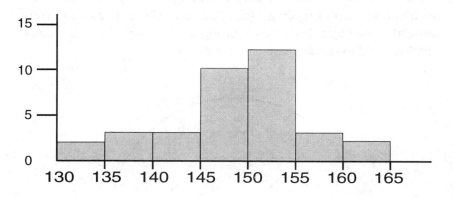

Graph of children's heights

Databases

A set of data which is regularly used and has been organised so that it can be retrieved is called a database. An example of a database is the class register, which usually contains personal information such as the names, addresses, telephone numbers and dates of birth of the pupils. A telephone directory, an address book and an author card index in the library are other common examples of databases. A computer database stores large amounts of information, which can be accessed, interrogated and printed out. Database applications for use in primary schools are often designed with built-in facilities to present information in the form of bar and line graphs and pie charts, which may be printed out when required.

Pie Charts

A pie chart can often show information in a more visually effective manner than a block diagram or bar chart. There is no requirement to teach pupils to construct them in Key Stage 2 although they should be taught to interpret them: it is relatively easy to see that the quantities are proportional to the corresponding areas of the sectors and to draw conclusions.

A computer can be used to draw a pie chart; for example, the graphing facility of database software specially designed for primary schools, such as Longman's Logotron Junior Pinpoint. Although unable to construct the chart by calculation of the angles the pupils produce the pie chart relating to the database with the computer.

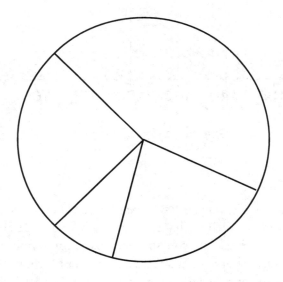

Pie chart

Statistical measures

Two important measures of a set of numerical data are the *average* value and the *spread or dispersion* of the values of the variable.

Imagine that there are two types of woodland accessible to a school. One was created twenty years ago by the Forestry Commission which planted a single species of conifer, probably for the woodpulp industry. The other woodland is ancient and consists of a variety of trees of widely differing age. The pupils decide to make a survey of the woods. One of the measures which they decide to take are the girths (circumferences) of the trees measured at a fixed height above the ground. They will not be able to measure all of the trees but will have to take a sample (perhaps every tenth tree in a small wood). When they have collected the data they calculate the average girth of the trees in each of the woods, and the spread of values. They compare them and discuss their findings and draw conclusions.

Averages

In fact, there are several different types of average, three of which are required to be taught in Key Stage 2: the mode, the median and mean. Pupils should be taught to calculate and use the different forms of average in appropriate, practical contexts. They should also be taught to calculate the range, which is a simple measure of the spread of values.

Averages – Mode

The mode is the most popular or common value of the variable. A manufacturer of shoes needs to know what sizes to make shoes and in what quantity. The most common size for men's shoes is 8, so that the factory should make more size 8 shoes than others. Size 8 is a sort of average shoe size for men because it is the most popular size — the mode. The mode is a measure which gives the sort of information which is useful to manufacturers of such things as potato crisps and ice-creams, where different flavours are offered. The manufacturer wishes to know the proportions in which to make the various flavours. It is also of use to providers of services such as railways, airlines and theatres which sell classes of ticket at various prices. The mode is the first sort of average which children meet and can understand and use.

In the distribution 'Our Pets' mentioned in Strand 5 of Number, pupils in Key Stage 1 discuss which animal is the most popular sort of pet.

Averages — Mean

The mean is calculated by finding the total of the observed values and dividing them by the number of the observed values. For example, given the set of eight numbers 15, 5, 4, 9, 12, 10, 20, 21 the mean is

$$\frac{(15+5+4+9+12+10+20+21)}{8} = 12$$

An advantage of the mean is that we can find important information by partly reversing the process of its calculation; for example, given that the mean of 20 observations is 2.5 we know that the total of the values of the observations is 2.5 x 20 = 50

The mean of the data relating to heights of 35 children, which appeared earlier is calculated by summing the heights and dividing by 35.

Averages — Median

The median is another sort of average: the central value of a set of data when arranged in order. If a football coach arranges his squad of 11 players in order of size, it is easy to pick out the median height: it is the height of the 6th player.

MEDIAN

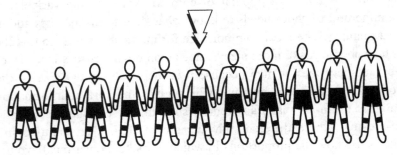

Footballers — the median height

If the team reserve player joins the squad there are now 12 present. There is now no middle height as there is an even number of players. In this case the median height is assumed to lie midway between the 6th and 7th value. The mean of those values is therefore taken.

MEDIAN

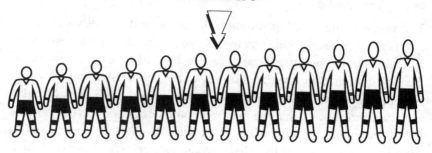

Footballers — the median height

The advantage of this kind of average is that any extreme values at either extreme end of the distribution, which might otherwise give rise to an unrepresentative measure of the average of the distribution, are neglected.

For example, the incomes (in numerical order) of twenty men could be as follows:

£35 000, £13 520, £13 510, £13 350, £13 290, £13 118, £12 980.

The sum of these incomes is £114 768

The mean is £114 768 ÷ 7

   = £16 395 (nearest whole number)

This value for the mean is quite unrepresentative as a measure of the income of the average member of this small group. It is too much influenced by the higher income of £35 000 and no member of the group actually receives an income quite like it. By contrast, the median is a much more representative and useful average value.

The median (of the seven salaries) is the 4th when arranged in order of size

   median salary = £13 350

Spread — Range

The range is the difference of the maximum and minimum values of the variable; for example, the age range of the passengers on a country bus is the age of the youngest subtracted from that of the eldest (note age is conventionally treated as a discrete variable: we are age six until our seventh birthday).

The range is the simplest measure of spread and is easily calculated and is easy to understand. The usefulness of the range as a measure of spread is limited because it only takes account of the extreme values of the distribution. Suppose that a survey of the numbers of people per car travelling over the Severn Bridge is taken at peak hour on a Monday morning and showed that the maximum number of persons per car was 6 and the minimum number, 1. The range of values is 5 but this is of little use; all we know is that there was at least one six-seater car which was full to capacity and at least one which had no passengers at all.

In some other circumstances, however, the range is a useful statistical measure; for example, in tidal measurements, where the range of high and low water marks is important, or in the case of the maximum-minimum thermometer. The comparison of the ranges of tree girth in the two woodland areas referred to earlier would show that the range of girths in the newly planted wood would be much smaller than that of the ancient wood. If a group of pupils was given the mean girth and range for each of the woodland areas, without prior knowledge of the subject of the survey, and asked to draw conclusions from the data they would be likely to conclude that the trees with the narrow range of girths had been planted at the same time.

Strand 3, Understanding and Using Probability

Probability is a new topic to primary schools. Following the latest review, the Key Stage 1 programme of study relating to probability has been deleted. The programme for teaching probability remains in Key Stage 2, but the level descriptions are unambitious for average and below average pupils and it appears that they are expected to gain very little from what is taught.

By the end of the key stage the majority of pupils, ie those attaining level 4, are expected to understand 'unlikely' and 'evens' whilst there is no expectation of understanding probability at all for those attaining level 3.

By contrast, the more able pupils, those who attain level 5 at the end of the key stage, are expected to have made good progress. By the end of the key stage, they have an understanding of probability as a number and the probability scale; are able to calculate probabilities based on equally likely outcomes and to carry out simple experiments with understanding.

In view of the low expectation for pupils of ordinary ability implicit in the level descriptions, the programme of study could be interpreted as being for the more able pupils, only. It would be regrettable if teachers restricted their work in probability for that reason.

The Probability Scale

Some events can be regarded as certain, eg that the sun will rise tomorrow; and others impossible: a giant rabbit will be elected during the next parliamentary by-election. The probability of an event is a numerical measure, between zero and one, of the *likelihood* of the event to happen. An impossible event is assigned a probability of 0 and a certainty a probability of 1, with all other degrees of probability taking values between, expressed either as fractions or decimals.

The probability, p, of an event is a number such that $0 \leq p \leq 1$.

An event which is likely to happen is considered to have a probability number much greater than 1/2 and an unlikely event has a probability number much less than 1/2. Where two events are equally likely, their probabilities are each 1/2 or 50%. Alternatively, they are said to have a fifty-fifty (or even) chance of happening.

Equally Likely Outcomes

When we roll a die, the possible outcomes are 1, 2, 3, 4, 5, 6. If the die is fair the outcomes are *equally likely* and, therefore, each outcome has the same probability. The equal likelihood is important as it enables us *to calculate* the probabilities.

The probability of one of a set of equally likely outcomes is defined as the number of ways in which it can occur, expressed as a fraction of the total number of outcomes possible. Some die-rolling examples follow to illustrate this.

The probability of getting a 'three' with a roll of a fair die is 1/6 since the number of ways 'three' can occur is one (only one three on a die) and the total number of possible outcomes is six (six faces on the die, a different number on each).

The probability of getting a square number with a single roll of a fair die is 2/6 since there are two square numbers (1 and 4) and six different, but equally likely, possible outcomes.

If a cube has two red faces and four white there are two possible outcomes – red and white. But they are not equally likely: the probabilities of getting a red or white face are different. Since there are two red faces and six faces and six faces in all, all equally likely, the probability of getting red is 2/6.

Another way of looking at it is this that there are six possible outcomes: R,R,W,W,W,W since there are two red and four white faces. The probability of a red face is, therefore, 2/6 and the probability of white is 4/6. Pupils should discuss why the probability of a red face up is not 1/2.

Experimental Probability

If a coin is fair the probabilities of the outcomes 'head' and 'tail' are equal. This can be verified by experiment to test for bias. We would expect the chance of getting a head or tail with a single toss of the coin to be evens. If we toss it ten times we might get six heads and four tails, say, rather than exactly five of each and would not be surprised by this. But this gives an experimental estimate of the probability of getting a head of 6/10 or 0.6 The number of trials is too small to be reliable. If we toss the coin twenty, fifty, a hundred, a thousand times, the more accurate the estimate will be and the closer to 1/2. Pupils should come to the conclusion that the larger the number of trials the greater the accuracy of the estimate is likely to be.

Pupils should learn to recognise circumstances where the probabilities of events are equally likely, and can be calculated, and other cases where estimates must be made by testing or experimenting.

Experiments are necessary to estimate probabilities where they cannot be calculated. Two examples follow.

1. Is a drawing pin more or less likely to land 'point up' than 'point down' when tossed?

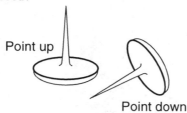

The drawing pin can land 'point up' or 'point down'. We have no way of knowing in advance what the probabilities of the two possible outcomes are but we may assume that they are not equally likely. If we make an experiment with 1000 trials or, more conveniently, one hundred trials, tossing ten drawing pins each trial and note the outcomes, we will be able to estimate of the probability that a drawing pin lands point up. An experiment was conducted to estimate the probability of the outcome 'point up'. The event 'point up' occurred in 590 out of 1000 tosses. The probability of 'point up' is therefore estimated as 590/1000 or 0.59.

2. A jar contains a large number of a mixture of two colours of coloured beads (or beans or whatever). In what proportion are the two colours mixed?

If the jar contains white and red beads, the chance that a bead selected at random will be red cannot be calculated, since the proportions of white and red are not known. An estimate can be made only by making an experiment: a sample of ten beads is removed at random, the proportions noted and the beans returned. The beads are shaken well and the trial is repeated so that 100 samples are inspected. When such an experiment was carried out a total of 1000 beads were sampled and 680 found to be white. An estimate of the probability that any bead drawn from this particular jar is white is, therefore, 680/1000 or 0.68.

PART 3
SOME FINAL OBSERVATIONS ON THE CURRICULUM

The innovations of the sixties and seventies which were identified by Elizabeth Biggs, HMI, in *Schools Council Bulletin No. 1*, brought algebraic structure and logic, probability and statistics and mathematical modelling to primary schools. Time has moved on and the algebraic structure, based on sets, has now virtually disappeared from the curriculum. The elements of the more traditional algebra (generalised arithmetic) which are still part of the revised National Curriculum programmes of study are mere vestiges of those originally proposed and of those of the first version of the Mathematics Order. Logic, in the form of sorting activities, with the purpose of developing early mathematical language and concepts, remains a part of the Key Stage 1 curriculum, albeit with much a diminished emphasis. Statistics (statistical methods) are even more firmly embedded than before, with importance strengthened by wide applicability to everyday life and across other subjects. The increasing sophistication and power of information technology and software enables more emphasis on statistical graphs – on interpretation of them as much as on construction.

The first attainment target (Using and Applying Mathematics) is based upon problem solving, communication, and the development of mathematical reasoning, argument and generalisation. The substance of the attainment target implicitly acknowledges the ideas that:

(i) children learn most effectively when engaged in practical activities which have meaning for them;

(ii) the purpose of learning mathematics, for most children, should empower them to solve practical problems and communicate their findings clearly;

(iii) mathematics is queen of the sciences as well as servant: above all it is about reason and truth.

The development of mathematical reasoning is back in fashion after more than a decade of neglect.

Although the programme of study for the secondary key stages is consistent with the growing importance of statistics and probability, Biggs' prophesy for probability in the primary curriculum has not yet been fulfilled.

The modelling approach to the teaching of number through the use of concrete referents and structured materials remains firmly established, even if teachers are still too much inclined to drop work with number apparatus too early. A diet of repetitive exercises and workcards, begun too early, at least partly accounts for the unsatisfactory standards of attainment in number work currently seen at the end of Key Stage 2.

In 1995, the first year in which pupils took the statutory SATs, only a minority of pupils (44%) reached the national standard in mathematics (level 4) set for their age. More than half of Year 6 pupils were not fully prepared, therefore, for the next stage of education. Many pupils have no proper grasp of fundamental number knowledge by the end of Year 6 – what Cockcroft called an 'at-homeness' with number (*Mathematics Counts*, HMSO, London, 1982). They are unlikely to recover in secondary school, as the secondary teachers have not been trained to teach number at this level and lack the necessary skills. As they move through secondary school, too many pupils lose their motivation to learn mathematics through constant and inevitable lack of success in the subject.

Extending opportunities

In the course of the book I have mentioned that there are no age-specific criteria defined in the National Curriculum. However, in the course of time, national curriculum levels are likely to emerge as pass/fail criteria. The benchmark end-of-key-stage levels (level 2, level 4) which were originally postulated as aspirations for the average child are being interpreted by the media and others as the 'expectation' for all children and that those who do not attain these levels will be considered to have failed. This new factor of expectation is likely to compel the raising of standards, not only in mathematics, but in all three core subjects.

Further material defined in the programmes of study extends the secondary Key Stage 3 and 4 programmes in order to challenge higher attaining pupils properly and provide for them to make progress commensurate with their capabilities. Regrettably, there is no equivalent of such extension material for Key Stage 2. There is plenty of scope for applying and consolidating existing knowledge in problem solving. Topics defined for the next key stage should also be included in plans, to enable the more capable pupils to progress to higher levels. Fruitful topics for extension work for Year 6 children could be:

(i) the development of abstract symbolic algebra and its application to define number patterns, especially in investigational work;

(ii) fractions, equivalent fractions and operations on fractions, especially in symbolic algebra;

(iii) directed numbers (positive and negative numbers) and operations on them, especially in algebra and graphs;

(iv) practical problems involving applying ideas of ratio and proportion, rate and compound measures, such as speed;

(v) angle properties of polygons;

(vi) practical statistical experiments yielding data which can be processed and illustrated in a variety of ways;

(vii) conducting practical probability experiments.

In conclusion

This has been a difficult book to write, not least because the National Curriculum Order was changed twice during the time of writing. It was also difficult to judge how much material to put into the chapters on the attainment targets given their overall scope and I am very conscious of the extreme brevity of the mention accorded to some topics; for example, fractions and percentages. Despite ommissions and brevity, I sincerely hope that it will be useful to primary school teachers everywhere. If it turns out so, then it will have been well worth the effort.

References

Alexander, R, Rose J, and Woodhead, C. *Curriculum Organisation and Classroom Practice in Primary Schools. A Discussion Paper.* (DES, 1992)

Bourgoin, J. *Arabic Geometrical Pattern and Design.* (Dover Publications, New York, 1973)

Cockcroft Committee. *Mathematics Counts.* (HMSO, 1982). (The Cockcroft Report)

DES. *Aspects of Primary Education: The Teaching and Learning of Mathematics.* (DES, HMSO 1989)

DES. *Mathematics in Primary Schools.* Schools Council Curriculum Bulletin No 10. (HMSO, London, 1972)

DFEE. *Code of Practice on the Identification and Assessment of Special Educational Needs.* (DFE, HMSO 1994)

DFEE. *Mathematics in the National Curriculum.* (DFE, HMSO 1995)

Elffers, J. *Tangram.* Penguin, 1971.

Harling, P. *100's of Ideas for Primary Maths.* (Hodder and Stoughton, London, 1991)

Howson, G. *National Curricula in Mathematics.* (The Mathematical Association, Bath Press, Avon, 1991)

OFSTED. *A review of inspection findings. Mathematics, 1993-94.* (OFSTED, HMSO. 1995)

OFSTED. *Curriculum Organisation and Clasroom Practice in Primary Schools. A follow-up Report.* (OFSTED, 1993)

OFSTED. *Mathematics. Key Stages 1,2,3 and 4. Fourth Year, 1992-93. The implementation of the curricular requirements of the Educational Reform Act. A report from the Office of OHMCI.* (OFSTED, HMSO, London, 1993)

OFSTED. *Science and Mathematics in Schools: a review* (OFSTED, HMSO, London, 1994)

OFSTED. *Subjects and Standards. Issues for school development arising from findings of Ofsted inspections, 1994-95.* (OFSTED, HMSO. 1996)

Skemp, R. *Mathematics in the Primary School* (Subjects in the Primary School). (Routledge, London, 1991)

Index